Gallery Books
Editor Peter Fallon

NEW COLLECTED POEMS

Derek Mahon

NEW
COLLECTED
POEMS

Gallery Books

New Collected Poems
is first published
simultaneously in paperback
and in a clothbound edition
on 12 May 2011.

The Gallery Press
Loughcrew
Oldcastle
County Meath
Ireland

www.gallerypress.com

ISBN 978 1 85235 512 8 *paperback*
       978 1 85235 513 5 *clothbound*
       978 1 85235 518 0 *limited, signed edition*

A CIP catalogue record for this book
is available from the British Library.

Contents

for Rory and Katie

Spring in Belfast

Walking among my own this windy morning
In a tide of sunlight between shower and shower,
I resume my old conspiracy with the wet
Stone and the unwieldy images of the squinting heart.
Once more, as before, I remember not to forget.

There is a perverse pride in being on the side
Of the fallen angels and refusing to get up.
We could *all* be saved by keeping an eye on the hill
At the top of every street, for there it is,
Eternally, if irrelevantly, visible —

But yield instead to the humorous formulae,
The spurious mystery in the knowing nod;
Or we keep sullen silence in light and shade,
Rehearsing our astute salvations under
The cold gaze of a sanctimonious God.

One part of my mind must learn to know its place.
The things that happen in the kitchen houses
And echoing back streets of this desperate city
Should engage more than my casual interest,
Exact more interest than my casual pity.

Glengormley

'Wonders are many and none is more wonderful than man'
Who has tamed the terrier, trimmed the hedge
And grasped the principle of the watering can.
Clothes pegs litter the window ledge
And the long ships lie in clover; washing lines
Shake out white linen over the chalk thanes.

Now we are safe from monsters, and the giants
Who tore up sods twelve miles by six
And hurled them out to sea to become islands
Can worry us no more. The sticks
And stones that once broke bones will not now harm
A generation of such sense and charm.

Only words hurt us now. No saint or hero,
Landing at night from the conspiring seas,
Brings dangerous tokens to the new era —
Their sad names linger in the histories.
The unreconciled, in their metaphysical pain,
Dangle from lamp posts in the dawn rain;

And much dies with them. I should rather praise
A worldly time under this worldly sky —
The terrier-taming, garden-watering days
Those heroes pictured as they struggled through
The quick noose of their finite being. By
Necessity, if not choice, I live here too.

Grandfather

They brought him in on a stretcher from the world,
Wounded but humorous, and he soon recovered.
Boiler-rooms, row upon row of gantries rolled
Away to reveal the landscape of a childhood
Only he can recapture. Even on cold
Mornings he is up at six with a block of wood
Or a box of nails, discreetly up to no good
Or banging round the house like a four-year-old —

Never there when you call. But after dark
You hear his great boots thumping in the hall
And in he comes, as cute as they come. Each night
His shrewd eyes bolt the door and wind the clock
Against the future, then his light goes out.
Nothing escapes him; he escapes us all.

September in Great Yarmouth

A woodwind whistles down the shore
Piping the stragglers home; the gulls
Snaffle and bolt their final mouthfuls.
Only the youngsters call for more.

Chimneys breathe and beaches empty,
Everyone queues for the inland cold —
Middle-aged parents growing old
And teenage kids becoming twenty.

Now the first few spots of rain
Spatter the sports page in the gutter.
Council workmen stab the litter.
You have sown and reaped; now sow again.

The band packs in, the banners drop,
The ice-cream stiffens in its cone.
The boatman lifts his megaphone:
'Come in, fifteen, your time is up.'

Carrowdore

(*at the grave of Louis MacNeice*)

Your ashes will not stir, even on this high ground,
However the wind tugs, the headstones shake.
This plot is consecrated, for your sake,
To what lies in the future tense. You lie
Past tension now, and spring is coming round
Igniting flowers on the peninsula.

Your ashes will not fly, however the winds roar
Through elm and bramble. Soon the biographies
And buried poems will begin to appear,
But we pause here to remember the lost life.
Maguire proposes a blackbird in low relief
Over the grave, and a phrase from Euripides.

Which suits you down to the ground, like this churchyard
With its play of shadow, its humane perspective.
Locked in the winter's fist, these hills are hard
As nails, yet soft and feminine in their turn
When fingers open and the hedges burn.
This, you implied, is how we ought to live —

The ironical, loving crush of roses against snow,
Each fragile, solving ambiguity. So
From the pneumonia of the ditch, from the ague
Of the blind poet and the bombed town you bring
The all-clear to the empty holes of spring,
Rinsing the choked mud, keeping the colours new.

First Love

This is a circling of itself and you —
A form of words, compact and compromise,
    Prepared in the false dawn of the half-true
Beyond which the shapes of truth materialize.
    This is a blind with sunlight filtering through.

This is a stirring in the silent hours,
As lovers do with thoughts they cannot frame
    Or leave, but bring to darkness like night flowers,
Words never choosing but the words choose them —
    Birds crowing, wind whistling off pale stars.

This is a night cry, neither here nor there,
A ghostly echo from the clamorous dead
    Who cried aloud in anger and despair
Outlasting stone and bronze, but took instead
    Their lost grins underground with them for ever.

This is at one remove, a substitute
For final answers; but the wise man knows
    To cleave to the one living absolute
Beyond paraphrase, and shun a shrewd repose.
    The words are aching in their own pursuit

To say 'I love you' out of indolence
As one might speak at sea without forethought,
    Drifting inconsequently among islands.
This is a way of airing my distraught
    Love of your silence; you are the soul of silence.

Bird Sanctuary

(for Jill Schlesinger)

Towards sleep I came
Upon the place again,
Its muted sea and tame
Eddying wind. The mist and rain
Come only after dark, and then
Steam out to sea at dawn.

I have erected
A bird sanctuary to hold
The loaded world in check.
This is where all my birds collect —
Gannet, puffin and kittiwake
All duly enrolled.

I live elsewhere —
In a city down the coast
Composed of earth and fire.
At night I walk beside the river
So that the elements of air
And water are not lost.

I expect great things
Of these angels of wind,
Females, males and fledglings.
The sudden whirring of their wings
Disturbs the noon, and midnight rings
With echoes from their island.

Will come a time
When they sit on the housetops
Shouting, thousands of them,
This is their own, their favourite dream
Beyond reason, beyond rhyme,
So that the heart stops.

De Quincey at Grasmere

Tonight the blessèd state, that long repose
Where time is measured
Not by the clock but by the hours
Of the wind; his seventh heaven when it snows
The valley under, and the frosty stars
Sing to his literary leisure.

Hearth rugs, a teapot and a quart
Decanter of laudanum —
Perihelion of paradise! No sort
Or condition of men but is the less human
For want of this: *mens sana
In corpore sano.*

Excellent as an antidote for toothache
And the busy streets. Wood crackles better
In a head removed, and fresh water
Springs wiselier in a heart that isn't sick.
And then the dreams came, and his children
Woke him every day at noon —

Until he cried out, 'I will sleep no more!',
And quit the hot sheets and the enormous
Apparitions dying on the floor.
He left the house,
Walked out to the sunlight on the hill
And heard, in the whispering-gallery of his soul,

His own small, urgent discord echoing back
From dark roads taken at random
And the restless thunder of London —
Where he had gone in his eighteenth year
And wandered Soho after dark
With Ann, looking for some such panacea.

Breton Walks

1. *Morning*
No doubt the creation was something like this —
A cold day breaking on silent stones,
Slower than time, spectacular only in size.
First there is darkness, then somehow light;
We call this day, and the other night,
And watch in vain for the second of sunrise.

Suddenly, near at hand, the click of a wooden shoe —
An old woman among the primeval shapes
Abroad in a field of light, sombrely dressed.
She calls good-day, since there are bad days too,
And her eyes go down. She has seen perhaps
Ten thousand dawns like this, and is not impressed.

2. *Man and Bird*
All fly away at my approach,
As they have done time out of mind,
And hide in the thicker leaves to watch
The shadowy presence of mankind.

My whistle-talk fails to disarm
Presuppositions of ill-will;
Although they rarely come to harm
The ancient fear is in them still.

Which irritates my *amour-propre*
As an enlightened alien
And renders yet more wide the gap
From their world to the world of men.

So perhaps they have something after all —
Either we shoot them out of hand
Or parody them with a bird-call
Neither of us can understand.

3. *After Midnight*
They are all round me in the dark
With claw-knives for my sleepy anarch —

Beasts of the field, birds of the air,
Their slit-eyes glittering everywhere.

I am man self-made, self-made man,
No small-talk now for those who ran

In and out of my grubby childhood.
We have grown up as best we could.

4. *Exit Molloy*
Now at the end I smell the smells of spring
Where in a dark ditch I lie wintering,
And the little town only a mile away
Happy and fatuous in the light of day.
A bell tolls gently. I should start to cry
But my eyes are closed and my face dry —
I am not important and I have to die.
Strictly speaking I am already dead
But still I can hear the birds sing on over my head.

A Portrait of the Artist

(*for Colin Middleton*)

Shivering in the darkness
Of pits, slag-heaps, turnip fields,
I gasp for light and life
Like a caged bird in springtime
Banging the bright bars.

Like a glow-worm I move among
The caged Belgian miners,
And the light on my forehead
Is the dying light of faith.
God gutters down to metaphor —

A subterranean tapping, light
Refracted in a glass of wine
As if through a church window,
Or a basin ringed with coal-dust
After the ritual evening bath.

Theo, I am discharged for being
Over-zealous, they call it,
And not looking the part.
In time I shall go south
And paint what I have seen —

A meteor of golden light
On chairs, faces and old boots,
Setting fierce fire to the eyes
Of sunflowers and fishing boats,
Each one a miner in disguise.

Day Trip to Donegal

We reached the sea in early afternoon,
Climbed stiffly out; there were things to be done,
Clothes to be picked up, friends to be seen.
As ever, the nearby hills were a deeper green
Than anywhere in the world, and the grave
Grey of the sea the grimmer in that enclave.

Down at the pier the boats gave up their catch,
A squirming glimmer of gills. They fetch
Ten times as much in the city as there,
And still the fish come in year after year —
Herring and mackerel, flopping about the deck
In attitudes of agony and heartbreak.

We left at eight, drove back the way we came,
The sea receding down each muddy lane.
Around midnight we changed down into suburbs
Sunk in a sleep no gale-force wind disturbs.
The time of year had left its mark
On frosty pavements glistening in the dark.

Give me a ring, goodnight, and so to bed . . .
That night the slow sea washed against my head,
Performing its immeasurable erosions —
Spilling into the skull, marbling the stones
That spine the very harbour wall,
Muttering its threat to villages of landfall.

At dawn I was alone far out at sea
Without skill or reassurance — nobody
To show me how, no promise of rescue —
Cursing my constant failure to take due
Forethought for this; contriving vain
Overtures to the vindictive wind and rain.

An Unborn Child

(*for Michael and Edna Longley*)

I have already come to the verge of
Departure; a month or so and
I shall be vacating this familiar room.
Its fabric fits me almost like a glove
While leaving latitude for a free hand.
I begin to put on the manners of the world
Sensing the splitting light above
My head, where in the silence I lie curled.

Certain mysteries are relayed to me
Through the dark network of my mother's body
While she sits sewing the white shrouds
Of my apotheosis. I know the twisted
Kitten that lies there sunning itself
Under the bare bulb, the clouds
Of goldfish mooning around upon the shelf.
In me these data are already vested;

I know them in my bones — bones which embrace
Nothing, for I am completely egocentric.
The pandemonium of encumbrances
Which will absorb me, mind and senses,
Intricacies of the maze and the rat-race,
I imagine only. Though they linger and,
Like fingers, stretch until the knuckles crack,
They cannot dwarf the dimensions of my hand.

I must compose myself at the nerve centre
Of this metropolis, and not fidget —
Although sometimes at night, when the city
Has gone to sleep, I keep in touch with it,
Listening to the warm red water
Racing in the rivers of my mother's body;
Or the moths, soft as eyelids, or the rain
Wiping its wet wings on the windowpane.

And sometimes too, in the small hours of the morning
When the dead filament has ceased to ring,
After the goldfish are dissolved in darkness
And the kitten has gathered itself up into a ball
Between the groceries and the sewing,
I slip the trappings of my harness
To range these hollows in discreet rehearsal
And, battering at the concavity of my caul,

Produce in my mouth the words, 'I want to live!' —
This my first protest, and shall be my last.
As I am innocent, everything I do
Or say is couched in the affirmative.
I want to see, hear, touch and taste
These things with which I am to be encumbered.
Perhaps I needn't worry. Give
Or take a day or two, my days are numbered.

Canadian Pacific

From famine, pestilence and persecution
Those gaunt forefathers shipped abroad to find
Rough stone of heaven beyond the western ocean
And staked their claim, and pinned their faith.
Tonight their children whistle through the dark;
Frost chokes the windows. They will not have heard
The wild geese flying south over the lakes
While the lakes harden beyond grief and anger —
The eyes fanatical, rigid the soft necks,
The great wings sighing with a nameless hunger.

Inis Oírr

(*for Eamon Grennan*)

A dream of limestone in sea-light
Where gulls have placed their perfect prints.
Reflection in that final sky
Shames vision into simple sight;
Into pure sense, experience.
Atlantic leagues away tonight,
Conceived beyond such innocence,
I clutch the memory still, and I
Have measured everything with it since.

After the Titanic

They said I got away in a boat
And humbled me at the inquiry. I tell you
    I sank as far that night as any
Hero. As I sat shivering on the dark water
    I turned to ice to hear my costly
Life go thundering down in a pandemonium of
    Prams, pianos, sideboards, winches,
Boilers bursting and shredded ragtime. Now I hide
    In a lonely house behind the sea
Where the tide leaves broken toys and hatboxes
    Silently at my door. The showers of
April, flowers of May mean nothing to me, nor the
    Late light of June, when my gardener
Describes to strangers how the old man stays in bed
    On seaward mornings after nights of
Wind, takes his morphine and will see no one. Then it is
    I drown again with all those dim
Lost faces I never understood, my poor soul
    Screams out in the starlight, heart
Breaks loose and rolls down like a stone.
    Include me in your lamentations.

Jail Journal

For several days I have been under
House arrest. My table has become
A sundial to its empty bottle.
With wise abandon
Lover and friend have gone.

In the window opposite
An old lady sits each afternoon
Talking to no one. I shout.
Either she is deaf or
She has reason.

I have books, provisions, running water
And a little stove. It wouldn't matter
If cars moved silently at night
And no light or laughter
Came from the houses down the street.

It's taking longer than almost anything —
But I know, when it's over
And back come friend and lover,
I shall forget it like a childhood illness
Or a sleepless night crossing.

No Rest for the Wicked

No rest for the wicked —
Curled up in armchairs
Or flat out on the floors
Of well-furnished apartments
Belonging to friends of friends,
We lie where we fell.

One more shiftless habit,
It joins the buttered books,
Stale loaves and wandering dishes,
The shirts in the oven
And the volcanic ashtray.
Forgive us, this is our way,

We were born to this —
Deckchairs, train corridors,
Greyhound bus stations,
Park benches, open boats
And wind-worried terraces
Of 19th-century Paris.

Forgive us, we mean well
To your wives' well-turned ankles,
Their anthropomorphic shoes.
We love your dying embers,
Your happy moonstruck bottles,
And we lie where we fell.

Back home at mid-morning
We wash, we change and drink
Coffee, perhaps we sing;
Then off we go once more,
Smiling our secret smile and only
Slightly the worse for wear.

Homecoming

Has bath and shave,
clean shirt etc.,
full of potatoes,
rested, yet
badly distraught
by six-hour flight
(Boston to Dublin)
drunk all night
with crashing bore
from Houston, Tex.,
who spoke at length
of guns and sex.
Bus into town
and, sad to say,
no change from when
he went away
two years ago.
Goes into bar,
affixes gaze
on evening star.
Skies change but not
souls change: behold
this is the way
the world grows old.
Scientists, birds,
we cannot start
at this late date
with a pure heart,
or having seen
the pictures plain
be ever innocent again.

A Dying Art

'That day would skin a fairy —
A dying art,' she said.
Not many left of the old trade.
Redundant and remote, they age
Gracefully in dark corners
With lamplighters, sailmakers
And native Manx speakers.

And the bone-handled knives with which
They earned their bread? My granny grinds
Her plug tobacco with one to this day.

Ecclesiastes

God, you could grow to love it, God-fearing, God-
    chosen purist little puritan that,
for all your wiles and smiles, you are (the
    dank churches, the empty streets,
the shipyard silence, the tied-up swings) and
    shelter your cold heart from the heat
of the world, from woman-inquisition, from the
    bright eyes of children. Yes, you could
wear black, drink water, nourish a fierce zeal
    with locusts and wild honey, and not
feel called upon to understand and forgive
    but only to speak with a bleak
afflatus, and love the January rains when they
    darken the dark doors and sink hard
into the Antrim hills, the shore, the heaped
    graves of your fathers. Bury that red
bandana and stick, that banjo; this is your
    country, close one eye and be king.
Your people await you, their heavy washing
    flaps for you in the housing estates —
a credulous people. God, you could do it, God
    help you, stand on a corner stiff
with rhetoric, promising nothing under the sun.

The Studio

You would think with so much going on outside
The deal table would make for the window,
The ranged crockery freak and wail
Remembering its dark origins, the frail
Oil-cloth, in a fury of recognitions,
Disperse in a thousand directions
And the simple bulb in the ceiling, honed
By death to a worm of pain, to a hair
Of heat, to a light snowflake laid
On a dark river at night — and wearied
Above all by the life-price of time
And the failure by only a few tenths
Of an inch but completely and for ever
Of the ends of a carefully drawn equator
To meet, sing and be one — abruptly
Roar into the floor.
                           But it
Never happens like that. Instead
There is this quivering silence
In which, day by day, the play
Of light and shadow (shadow mostly)
Repeats itself, though never exactly.

This is the all-purpose bed-, work- and bedroom.
Its mourning faces are cracked porcelain only quicker,
Its knuckles doorknobs only lighter,
Its occasional cries of despair
A function of the furniture.

Aran

(for Tom and Peggy Mac Intyre)

He is earthed to his girl, one hand fastened
In hers, and with his free hand listens,
An earphone, to his own version
Singing the darkness into the light.
I close the pub door gently and step out
Into the yard and the song goes out
And a gull creaks off from the tin roof
Of an outhouse, planing over the ocean,
Circling now with a hoarse inchoate
Screaming the bone fields of its vision.
God, that was the way to do it,
Hand-clasping, echo-prolonging poet!

Scorched with a fearful admiration,
Walking over the nacreous sand,
I dream myself to that tradition
Generations off the land —
One hand to an ear for the vibration,
The far wires, the reverberation
Down light-years of the imagination,
A loved hand in the other hand.

The long glow springs from the dark soil, however —
No marsh-light holds a candle to this;
Unearthly still in its white weather
A crack-voiced rock-marauder, scavenger, fierce
Friend to no slant fields or the sea either,
Folds back over the forming waters.

A Tolerable Wisdom

You keep the cold from the body, the cold from the mind.
Heartscloth, soulswool, without you there would be
Short shrift for the pale beast in a winter's wind,
Too swift exposure by too harsh a sea.
Cold I have known, its sports pages adrift
Past frozen dodgems in the amusement park,
One crumpled Gauloise thumbing a late lift
Where Paris flamed on the defining dark.

You've heard the gravel at the window, seen
A lost figure unmanned by closing time.
More honour to you that you took him in,
Fed buns and cocoa, sweetness, the sought dream
Of warmth and light against your listening skin,
And rocked him to a tolerable wisdom.

Two Songs for Doreen

1. *His Song*
Months on, you hold me still;
at dawn, bright-rising, like a hill-
horizon, gentle, kind with rain
and the primroses of April.
I shall never know them again
but still your bright shadow
puts out its shadow, daylight, on
the shadows I lie with now.

2. *Her Song*
A hundred men imagine
love when I drink wine,
and then I begin to think
of your words and mine.
The hills are silent now
where the snow lies fresh,
and my love like the sloe-
blossom on a blackthorn bush.

An Image from Beckett

In that instant
There was a sea, far off,
As bright as lettuce,

A northern landscape
And a huddle
Of houses along the shore.

Also, I think, a white
Flicker of gulls
And washing hung to dry —

The poignancy of those
Back yards! — and the gravedigger
Putting aside his forceps.

Then the hard boards
And darkness once again.
But in that instant

I was struck by the
Sweetness and light,
The sweetness and light,

Imagining what grave
Cities, what lasting monuments,
Given the time.

They will have buried
Our great-grandchildren, and theirs,
Beside us by now

With a subliminal batsqueak
Of reflex lamentation.
Our knuckle bones

Litter the rich earth
Changing, second by second,
To civilizations.

It was good while it lasted,
And if it only lasted
The Biblical span

Required to drop six feet
Through a glitter of wintry light,
There is No One to blame.

Still, I am haunted
By that landscape,
The soft rush of its winds,

The uprightness of its
Utilities and schoolchildren —
To whom in my will,

This, I have left my will.
I hope they have time,
And light enough, to read it.

A Stone Age Figure Far Below

(for Bill McCormack)

Through heaving heather, fallen stones
From the wrecked piles of burial cairns
As they fly in over the moors —
Racing about in cloud shadow,
A Stone Age figure far below
Wildly gesticulating as if
He sees, at last, a sign of life
Or damns them to hell-fires.

When they come with sticks, binoculars, whistles,
Blankets and flasks, they will find him dead —
Unkempt, authentic, furnace-eyed
And dead, and his heavy flint hearthstones
Littered with dung and animal bones;

Or a local resident out for a walk
In tweeds and a hunting hat. 'You must be
Mad,' he will say, 'to suppose this rock
Could accommodate life indefinitely.
Nobody comes here now but me.'

J. P. Donleavy's Dublin

'When you stop to consider
the days spent dreaming of a future
and say then, that was my life' —

for the days are long:
from the first milk van
to the last shout in the night
an eternity. But the weeks go by
like birds; and the years, the years
fly past anticlockwise
like clock hands in a bar mirror.

Lives

(for Seamus Heaney)

First time out
I was a torc of gold
And wept tears of the sun.

That was fun
But they buried me
In the earth two thousand years

Till a labourer
Turned me up with a pick
In eighteen fifty-four.

Once I was an oar
But stuck in the shore
To mark the place of a grave

When the lost ship
Sailed away. I thought
Of Ithaca, but soon decayed.

The time that I liked
Best was when
I was a bump of clay

In a Navaho rug,
Put there to mitigate
The too god-like

Perfection of that
Merely human artifact.
I served my maker well —

He lived long
To be struck down in
Denver by an electric shock

The night the lights
Went out in Europe
Never to shine again.

So many lives,
So many things to remember!
I was a stone in Tibet,

A tongue of bark
At the heart of Africa
Growing darker and darker . . .

It all seems
A little unreal now,
Now that I am

An anthropologist
With my own
Credit card, dictaphone,

Army-surplus boots
And a whole boatload
Of photographic equipment.

I know too much
To be anything any more;
And if in the distant

Future someone
Thinks he has once been me
As I am today,

Let him revise
His insolent ontology
Or teach himself to pray.

Rage for Order

Somewhere beyond
The scorched gable end
And the burnt-out
Buses there is a poet indulging his
Wretched rage for order —

Or not as the case
May be, for his
Is a dying art,
An eddy of semantic scruple
In an unstructurable sea.

He is far
From his people,
And the fitful glare
Of his high window is as
Nothing to our scattered glass.

His posture is
Grandiloquent and
Deprecating, like this,
His diet ashes,
His talk of justice and his mother

The rhetorical
Device of a Claudian emperor —
Nero if you prefer,
No mother there;
And this in the face of love, death and the wages of the poor.

If he is silent
It is the silence
Of enforced humility,
If anxious to be heard
It is the anxiety of a last word

When the drums start —
For his is a dying art.
Now watch me
As I make history,
Watch as I tear down

To build up
With a desperate love,
Knowing it cannot be
Long now till I have need of his
Terminal ironies.

As It Should Be

We hunted the mad bastard
Through bog, moorland, rock, to the starlit west
And gunned him down in a blind yard
Between ten sleeping lorries
And an electricity generator.

Let us hear no idle talk
Of the moon in the Yellow River:
The air blows softer since his departure.

Since his tide-burial during school hours
Our children have known no bad dreams.
Their cries echo lightly along the coast.

This is as it should be.
They will thank us for it when they grow up
To a world with method in it.

Consolations of Philosophy

When we start breaking up in the wet darkness
And the rotten boards fall from us, and the ribs
Crack under the constriction of tree-roots
And the seasons slip from the fields unknown to us,

Oh, then there will be the querulous complaining
From citizens who had never dreamt of this —
Who, shaken to the bone in their stout boxes
By the latest bright cars, will not inspect them

And, kept awake by the tremors of new building,
Will not be there to comment. When the broken
Wreath bowls are speckled with rainwater
And the grass grows wild for want of a caretaker,

There will be time to live through in the mind
The lives we might have lived, and get them right;
To lie in silence listening to the wind
Mourn for the living through the livelong night.

I Am Raftery

I am Raftery, hesitant and confused among the
loud-voiced graduate students and inter-
changeable instructors; were it not for the
nice wives who do the talking I would have
run out of hope some time ago, and of love.
I have traded-in my 'simplistic maunderings'
for a slick imagery and wry dissimulation.
Death is near, I have come of age, I doubt if
I shall survive another New England winter.
Jameson, plenty of water. Is it empty
pockets I play to? Not on your life:
they ring with a bright inflationary music —
two seminars a week and my own place reserved
in the record library. Look at me now,
my back to the wall, taking my cue from
a grinning disc jockey between commercials.

Beyond Howth Head

(for Jeremy Lewis)

The wind that blows these words to you
bangs nightly off the black-and-blue
Atlantic, hammering in its haste
dark doors of the declining west
whose rock-built houses year by year
collapse, whose children disappear
(no homespun cottage industries'
embroidered cloths will patch up these

lost townlands on the crumbling shores
of Europe); shivers the dim stars
in rainwater, and spins a single
garage sign behind the shingle.
Fresh from Long Island or Cape Cod
night music finds the lightning rod
of young girls coming from a dance
(you thumbs a lift and takes your chance)

and shakes the radio sets that play
from Carraroe to Dublin Bay
where, bored to tears by Telefís,
vox populi vox Dei, we reach
with twinkling importunity
for good news on the BBC,
our heliotropic Birnam Wood
reflecting an old gratitude.

What can the elders say to this?
The young must kiss and then must kiss
and so by this declension fall
to scrawl the writing on the wall.
A little learning in a parked
Volkswagen torches down the dark
and soon disperses tired belief
with an empiric *joie de vivre*.

The pros outweigh the cons that glow
from Beckett's bleak reductio —
and who would trade self-knowledge for
a prelapsarian metaphor,
love-play of the ironic conscience
for a prescriptive innocence?
'Lewde libertie', whose midnight work
disturbed the peace of Co. Cork

and fired Kilcolman's windows when
the Ulster chieftains looked to Spain,
come and inspire us once again!
But take a form that sheds for love
that prim conventual disdain
the world beyond knows nothing of;
and flash, an *aisling*, through the dawn
where Yeats's hill-men still break stone.

I woke this morning (March) to hear
church bells of Monkstown through the roar
of waves round the Martello tower
and thought of the lost swans of Lir
when Kemoc rang the Christian bell
to crack the fourth-dimensional
world picture of a vanished aeon,
making them human once again.

It calls as oddly through the wild
eviscerations of the troubled
waters between us and North Wales
where Lycid's ghost for ever sails
(unbosomings of seaweed, wrack,
industrial bile, a boot from Blackpool,
contraceptives deftly tied
with best regards from Merseyside)

and tinkles with as blithe a sense
of man's cosmic significance
who wrote his world from broken stone,
installed his word-God on the throne
and placed, in Co. Clare, a sign:
'Stop here and see the sun go down.'
Meanwhile, for a word's sake, the plastic
bombs go off around Belfast;

from the unquiet Cyclades
a Greek poet consults the skies
where sleepless, cold, computed stars
in random sequence light the bars;
and everywhere the ground is thick
with the dead sparrows rhetoric
demands as fictive sacrifice
to prove its substance in our eyes.

Roaring, its ten-lane highways pitch
their naked bodies in the ditch
where once Molloy, uncycled, heard
thin cries of a surviving bird;
and Washington, its grisly aim
to render the whole earth the same,
sends the B-52s to make it
safe for Chase and the stock market.

Spring lights the country; from a thousand
dusty corners, house by house,
from under beds and vacuum cleaners,
empty Calor Gas containers,
bread bins, car seats, crates of stout,
the first flies cry to be let out,
to cruise a kitchen, find a door
and die clean in the open air

whose smokeless clarity distils
a chisel's echo in the hills
as if some Noah, weather-wise,
could read a deluge in clear skies.
But nothing ruffles the wind's breath —
this peace is the great peace of death
or *l'outre-tombe*; make no noise,
the foxes have quit Clonmacnoise.

I too, uncycled, might exchange,
since 'we are changed by what we change',
my forkful of the general mess
for hazelnuts and watercress
like one of those old hermits who,
less virtuous than some, withdrew
from the world circles people make
to a small island in a lake.

Chomēi at Tōyama, his blanket
hemp, his character a rank
not-to-be-trusted river mist,
events in Kyōto all grist
to the mill of a harsh irony,
since we are seen by what we see;
Thoreau like ice among the trees
and Spenser, 'farre from enimyes',

might serve as models for a while
but to return in greater style.
Centripetal, the hot world draws
its children in with loving paws
from rock and heather, rain and sleet
with only Calor Gas for heat
and spins them at the centre where
they have no time to know despair.

The light that left you streaks the walls
of Georgian houses, pubs, cathedrals,
coasters moored below Butt Bridge
and old men at the water's edge
where Anna Livia, breathing free,
weeps silently into the sea,
her tiny sorrows mingling with
the wandering waters of the earth.

And here I close; for look, across
dark waves where bell-buoys dimly toss
the Baily winks beyond Howth Head
and sleep calls from the silent bed;
while the moon drags her kindred stones
among the rocks and the strict bones
of the drowned, and I put out the light
on shadows of the encroaching night.

Afterlives

(*for James Simmons*)

I

I wake in a dark flat
To the soft roar of the world.
Pigeons neck on the white
Roofs as I draw the curtains
And look out over London
Rain-fresh in the morning light.

This is our element, the bright
Reason on which we rely
For the long-term solutions.
The orators yap, and guns
Go off in a back street;
But the faith doesn't die

That in our time these things
Will amaze the literate children
In their non-sectarian schools
And the dark places be
Ablaze with love and poetry
When the power of good prevails.

What middle-class shits we are
To imagine for one second
That our privileged ideals
Are divine wisdom, and the dim
Forms that kneel at noon
In the city not ourselves.

2

I am going home by sea
For the first time in years.
Somebody thumbs a guitar
On the dark deck, while a gull
Dreams at the masthead,
The moon-splashed waves exult.

At dawn the ship trembles, turns
In a wide arc to back
Shuddering up the grey lough
Past lightship and buoy,
Slipway and dry dock
Where a naked bulb burns;

And I step ashore in a fine rain
To a city so changed
By five years of war
I scarcely recognize
The places I grew up in,
The faces that try to explain.

But the hills are still the same
Grey-blue above Belfast.
Perhaps if I'd stayed behind
And lived it bomb by bomb
I might have grown up at last
And learnt what is meant by home.

Leaves

The prisoners of infinite choice
Have built their house
In a field below the wood
And are at peace.

It is autumn, and dead leaves
On their way to the river
Scratch like birds at the windows
Or tick on the road.

Somewhere there is an afterlife
Of dead leaves,
A forest filled with an infinite
Rustling and sighing.

Somewhere in the heaven
Of lost futures
The lives we might have led
Have found their own fulfilment.

Homage to Malcolm Lowry

For gear your typewriter and an old rugby boot,
The voyage started, clearly, when you were born
That danced those empty bottles. When you set out
On a round-the-cosmos trip with a furious Muse
Or lay sweating on a hotel bed in Veracruz,
Did you not think you had left that pool astern
Where a soul might bathe and be clean or slake its drought?
In any case, your deportment in those seas
Was faultless. Lightning-blind, you, tempest-torn
At the poles of our condition, did not confuse
The Gates of Ivory with the Gates of Horn.

A Curious Ghost

While your widow clatters water into a kettle
You lie at peace in your tropical grave —
A sea captain who died at sea, almost.
Lost voyager, what would you think of me,
Husband of your fair daughter but impractical?
You stare from the mantelpiece, a curious ghost
In your peaked cap, as we sit down to tea.
The bungalows still signal to the sea,
Rain wanders the golf course as in your day,
The river still flows past the distillery
And a watery sun shines on Portballintrae.

I think we would have had a lot in common —
Alcohol and the love of one woman
Certainly; but I failed the eyesight test
When I tried for the Merchant Navy,
And lapsed into this lyric lunacy.
When you lost your balance like Li Po
They found unfinished poems in your sea-chest.

The Snow Party

(*for Louis Asekoff*)

Bashō, coming
To the city of Nagoya,
Is asked to a snow party.

There is a tinkling of china
And tea into china;
There are introductions.

Then everyone
Crowds to the window
To watch the falling snow.

Snow is falling on Nagoya
And farther south
On the tiles of Kyōto;

Eastward, beyond Irago,
It is falling
Like leaves on the cold sea.

Elsewhere they are burning
Witches and heretics
In the boiling squares,

Thousands have died since dawn
In the service
Of barbarous kings;

But there is silence
In the houses of Nagoya
And the hills of Ise.

The Last of the Fire Kings

I want to be
Like the man who descends
At two milk churns

With a bulging
String bag and vanishes
Where the lane turns,

Or the man
Who drops at night
From a moving train

And strikes out over the fields
Where fireflies glow,
Not knowing a word of the language.

Either way, I am
Through with history —
Who lives by the sword

Dies by the sword.
Last of the fire kings, I shall
Break with tradition and

Die by my own hand
Rather than perpetuate
The barbarous cycle.

Five years I have reigned
During which time
I have lain awake each night

And prowled by day
In the sacred grove
For fear of the usurper,

Perfecting my cold dream
Of a place out of time,
A palace of porcelain

Where the frugivorous
Inheritors recline
In their rich fabrics
Far from the sea.

But the fire-loving
People, rightly perhaps,
Will not countenance this,

Demanding that I inhabit,
Like them, a world of
Sirens, bin-lids
And bricked-up windows —

Not to release them
From the ancient curse
But to die their creature and be thankful.

The Antigone Riddle

Elocution, logic, political science,
Antibiotics, do-it-yourself,
And a plover flops in his oil slick.

Shy minerals contract at the sound of his voice,
Cod point in silence when his bombers pass,
And the windfall waits
In silence for his departure
Before it drops in
Silence to the long grass.

Gipsies

I've watched the dark police
rocking your caravans
to wreck the crockery
and wry thoughts of peace
you keep there on waste
ground beside motorways
where the snow lies late
(all this on television)
and am ashamed; fed,
clothed, housed and ashamed.
You might be interested
to hear, though, that on
stormy nights our strong
double glazing groans with
foreknowledge of death,
the fridge with a great wound,
and not surprised to know
the fate you have so long
endured is ours also:
the cars are piling up.
I listen to the wind
and file receipts; the heap
of scrap metal in my
garden grows daily.

The Mayo Tao

I have abandoned the dream kitchens for a low fire
and a prescriptive literature of the spirit;
a storm snores on the desolate sea.
The nearest shop is four miles away —
when I walk there through the shambles
of the morning for tea and firelighters
the mountain paces me in a snow-lit silence.
My days are spent in conversation
with deer and blackbirds;
at night fox and badger gather at my door.
I have stood for hours
watching a salmon doze in the tea-gold dark,
for months listening to the sob story
of a stone in the road, the best,
most monotonous sob story I have ever heard.

I am an expert on frost crystals
and the silence of crickets, a confidant
of the stinking shore, the stars in the mud —
there is an immanence in these things
which drives me, despite my scepticism,
almost to the point of speech,
like sunlight cleaving the lake mist at morning
or when tepid water
runs cold at last from the tap.

I have been working for years
on a four-line poem
about the life of a leaf;
I think it might come out right this winter.

Light Music

1. *Architecture*
Twinkletoes in the ballroom,
light music in space.

2. *History*
The blinking puddles
reflected day-long
twilights of misery.

Smoke rose in silence
to the low sky.

3. *Negatives*
Gulls in a rain-dark cornfield,
crows on a sunlit sea.

4. *North Sea*
The terminal light of beaches,
pebbles speckled with oil;
old tins at the tide-line
where a gull blinks on a pole.

5. *Please*
I built my house
in a forest far
from the venal roar.

Somebody please
beat a path
to my door.

6. *Rory*
He leads me into
a grainy twilight
of old photographs.

The sun is behind us,
his shadow in mine.

7. *Spring*
Dawn light pearling the branches,
petals freckling the mould,
and the stereo birds.

It is time for the nymphs,
a glimpse of skin in the woods.

8. *Twilight*
A stone at the roadside
watches snow fall
on the silent gate lodge.

Later the gate shuts
with a clanging of bars;
the stone is one with the stars.

9. *Mozart*
The Clarinet Concerto
in A, K.622,
the second movement.

Turn it up
so they can hear
on the other planets!

10. *Morphology*
Beans and foetuses,
brains and cauliflowers;
in a shaft of sunlight
a dust of stars.

11. *Enter*
The steel regrets the lock,
a word will open the rock,
the wood awaits your knock.

12. *Dawn Moon*
A slip of soap in the sky,
I do my faint shining
in the golden dawn
of an alien dispensation.

13. *Elpenor*
Edacity in the palace
and in the sandy timber
of my crumbling monument,
its lengthening shadow
pointing towards home.

14. *East Strand*
Tedium of sand and sea —
then at the white rocks
a little girl fleetingly,
blazer and ankle-socks.

Sand drifts from a rock
like driven snow, and one
gull attentive to my walk
obscures the winter sun.

15. *Absence*
I wake at night
in a house white
with moonlight.

Somewhere my son,
his vigour, his laughter;
somewhere my daughter.

16. *Waterfront*
I cover the waterfront,
its fish and chips,
while others go
down to the sea in ships.

17. *Outside*
The sculpted bird bath and the pine,
the postbox and the telephone line.

18. *Donegal*
The vast clouds migrate
above turf-stacks
and a dangling gate.

A tiny bike squeaks
into the wind.

19. *Smoke*
Vertical, horizontal,
the smoke of last resorts.

20. *Rogue Leaf*
Believe it or not
I hung on all winter
outfacing wind and snow.

Now that spring
comes and the birds sing
I am letting go.

21. *Revelation*
A colour the fish know
we do not know so
long have we been ashore.

When that colour
shines in the rainbow
there will be no more sea.

22. *Flying*
A wand of sunlight
touches the rush hour
like the finger of heaven.

A land of cumulus
seen from above
is the life to come.

Nostalgias

The chair squeaks in a high wind,
Rain falls from its branches;
The kettle yearns for the mountain,
The soap for the sea.
In a tiny stone church
On a desolate headland
A lost tribe is singing 'Abide with Me'.

Ford Manor

Even on the quietest days the distant
growl of cars remains persistent,
reaching us in this airy box
we share with the fieldmouse and the fox;
but she drifts in maternity blouses
among crack-paned greenhouses —
a pregnant Muse in love with life,
part child, part mother, and part wife.

Even on the calmest nights the fitful
prowl of planes is seldom still
where Gatwick tilts to guide them home
from Tokyo, Nice, New York or Rome;
yet even today the earth disposes
bluebells, roses and primroses,
the dawn throat-whistle of a thrush
deep in the dripping lilac bush.

Penshurst Place

The bright drop quivering on a thorn
in the rich silence after rain,
lute music in the orchard aisles,
the paths ablaze with daffodils,
intrigue and venery in the air
à l'ombre des jeunes filles en fleurs,
the iron hand and the velvet glove —
come live with me and be my love.

A pearl face numinously bright
shining in silence of the night,
a muffled crash of smouldering logs,
bad dreams of courtiers and of dogs,
the Spanish ships around Kinsale,
the screech-owl and the nightingale,
the falcon and the turtle dove —
come live with me and be my love.

The Mute Phenomena

(*after Nerval*)

Your great mistake is to disregard the satire
Bandied among the mute phenomena.
Be strong if you must, your brisk hegemony
Means fuck-all to the somnolent sunflower
Or the extinct volcano. What do you know
Of the revolutionary theories advanced
By turnips, or the sex life of cutlery?
Everything is susceptible, Pythagoras said so.

An ordinary common-or-garden brick wall, the kind
For talking to or banging your head on,
Resents your politics and bad draughtsmanship.
God is alive and lives under a stone;
Already in a lost hubcap is conceived
The ideal society which will replace our own.

The Banished Gods

Paros, far-shining star of dark-blue Earth,
    Reverts to the sea its mother.
      The tiny particles,
    Sand grains and marble dust,
Panic into the warm brine together.

Near the headwaters of the longest river
    There is a forest clearing,
      A dank, misty place
    Where light stands in columns
And birds sing with a noise like paper tearing.

Far from land, far from the trade routes,
    In an unbroken dream-time
      Of penguin and whale
    The seas sigh to themselves
Reliving the days before the days of sail.

Down a dark lane at the back of beyond
    A farm dog lies by a dead fire
      Dreaming of nothing
    While a window goes slowly grey
Brightening a laid table and hung clothing.

Where the wires end the moor seethes in silence,
    Scattered with scree, primroses,
      Feathers and faeces;
    It shelters the hawk and hears
In dreams the forlorn cries of lost species.

It is here that the banished gods are in hiding,
    Here they sit out the centuries
      In stone, water
    And the hearts of trees,
Lost in a reverie of their own natures —

Of zero-growth economics and seasonal change
In a world without cars, computers
    Or nuclear skies,
Where thought is a fondling of stones
And wisdom a five-minute silence at moonrise.

A Refusal to Mourn

He lived in a small farmhouse
At the edge of a new estate.
The trim gardens crept
To his door, and car engines
Woke him before dawn
On dark winter mornings.

All day there was silence
In the bright house. The clock
Ticked on the kitchen shelf,
Cinders moved in the grate,
And a warm briar gurgled
When the old man talked to himself;

But the doorbell seldom rang
After the milkman went,
And if a shirt-hanger
Knocked in an open wardrobe
That was a strange event
To be pondered on for hours

While the wind thrashed about
In the back garden, raking
The tin roof of the hen-house,
And swept clouds and gulls
Eastwards over the lough
With its flap of tiny sails.

Once a week he would visit
An old shipyard crony,
Inching down to the road
And the blue country bus
To sit and watch sun-dappled
Branches whipping the windows

While the long evening shed
Weak light in his empty house,
On the photographs of his dead
Wife and their six children
And the Missions to Seamen angel
In flight above the bed.

'I'm not long for this world,'
Said he on our last evening,
'I'll not last the winter,'
And grinned, straining to hear
Whatever reply I made;
And died the following year.

In time the astringent rain
Of those parts will clean
The words from his gravestone
In the crowded cemetery
That overlooks the sea
And his name be mud once again

And his boilers lie like tombs
In the mud of the sea bed
Till the next ice age comes
And the earth he inherited
Is gone like Neanderthal Man
And no records remain.

But the secret bred in the bone
On the dawn strand survives
In other times and lives,
Persisting for the unborn
Like a claw-print in concrete
After the bird has flown.

A Disused Shed in Co. Wexford

Let them not forget us, the weak souls among the asphodels.
— Seferis, *Mythistorema*

(for J. G. Farrell)

Even now there are places where a thought might grow —
Peruvian mines, worked out and abandoned
To a slow clock of condensation,
An echo trapped for ever, and a flutter
Of wildflowers in the lift-shaft,
Indian compounds where the wind dances
And a door bangs with diminished confidence,
Lime crevices behind rippling rain barrels,
Dog corners for bone burials;
And in a disused shed in Co. Wexford,

Deep in the grounds of a burnt-out hotel,
Among the bathtubs and the washbasins
A thousand mushrooms crowd to a keyhole.
This is the one star in their firmament
Or frames a star within a star.
What should they do there but desire?
So many days beyond the rhododendrons
With the world waltzing in its bowl of cloud,
They have learnt patience and silence
Listening to the rooks querulous in the high wood.

They have been waiting for us in a foetor
Of vegetable sweat since civil war days,
Since the gravel-crunching, interminable departure
Of the expropriated mycologist.
He never came back, and light since then
Is a keyhole rusting gently after rain.
Spiders have spun, flies dusted to mildew
And once a day, perhaps, they have heard something —
A trickle of masonry, a shout from the blue
Or a lorry changing gear at the end of the lane.

There have been deaths, the pale flesh flaking
Into the earth that nourished it;
And nightmares, born of these and the grim
Dominion of stale air and rank moisture.
Those nearest the door grow strong —
'Elbow room! Elbow room!'
The rest, dim in a twilight of crumbling
Utensils and broken pitchers, groaning
For their deliverance, have been so long
Expectant that there is left only the posture.

A half century, without visitors, in the dark —
Poor preparation for the cracking lock
And creak of hinges; magi, moonmen,
Powdery prisoners of the old regime,
Web-throated, stalked like triffids, racked by drought
And insomnia, only the ghost of a scream
At the flash-bulb firing-squad we wake them with
Shows there is life yet in their feverish forms.
Grown beyond nature now, soft food for worms,
They lift frail heads in gravity and good faith.

They are begging us, you see, in their wordless way,
To do something, to speak on their behalf
Or at least not to close the door again.
Lost people of Treblinka and Pompeii!
'Save us, save us,' they seem to say,
'Let the god not abandon us
Who have come so far in darkness and in pain.
We too had our lives to live.
You with your light meter and relaxed itinerary,
Let not our naive labours have been in vain!'

Autobiographies

(for Maurice Leitch)

1. *The Home Front*
While the frozen armies trembled
At the gates of Leningrad
They took me home in a taxi
And put me in my cot,
And there I slept again
With siren and black-out;

And slept under the stairs
Beside the light meter
When bombs fell on the city;
So I never saw the sky
Ablaze with a fiery glow,
Searchlights roaming the stars.

But I do remember one time
(I must have been four then)
Being held up to the window
For a victory parade —
Soldiers, sailors and airmen
Lining the Antrim Road;

And later hide-and-seek
Among the air-raid shelters,
The last ration coupons,
Oranges and bananas,
Slick sidecaps and badges
And packets of Lucky Strike.

Gracie Fields on the radio!
Americans in the art-deco
Teashops! The released Jews
Blinking in shocked sunlight . . .
A male child in a garden
Clutching the *Empire News.*

2. *The Lost Girls*

'In ancient shadows and twilights
Where childhood had strayed'
I ran round in the playground
Of Skegoneil Primary School
During the lunch break,
Pretending to be a plane.

For months I would dawdle home
At a respectful distance
Behind the teacher's daughter,
Eileen Boyd, who lived
In a house whose back garden
Was visible from my window.

I watched her on summer evenings,
A white dress picking flowers,
Her light, graceful figure
Luminous and remote.
We never exchanged greetings;
Her house was bigger than ours.

She married an older man
And went to live in Kenya.
Perhaps she is there still
Complaining about the 'natives'.
It would be nice to know;
But who can re-live their lives?

Eileen Boyd, Hazel and Heather
Thompson, Patricia King —
The lost girls in a ring
On a shadowy school playground
Like nymphs dancing together
In a forgotten spring.

3. *The Last Resort*
Salad-and-sand sandwiches
And dead gulls on the beach;
Ice-cream in the Arcadia,
Rain lashing the windows;
Dull days in the harbour,
Sunday mornings in church.

One hot July fortnight
In the Strandmore Hotel
I watched the maid climb
The stairs, and went to my room
Quivering with excitement,
Aroused for the first time.

Years later, the same dim
Resort has grown dimmer
As if some centrifugal
Force, summer by summer,
Has moved it ever farther
Towards a far horizon.

The guest-houses are crazy
For custom; but the risen
People are playing football
On the sands of Tenerife,
Far from the unrelaxing
Scenes of sectarian strife.

Yet the place really existed
And still can crack a smile
Should a sunbeam pick out
Your grimy plastic cup
And consecrate your vile
Bun with its parting light.

4. *The Bicycle*
There was a bicycle, a fine
Raleigh with five gears
And racing handlebars.
It stood at the front door
Begging to be mounted;
The frame shone in the sun.

I became like a character
In *The Third Policeman*, half
Human, half bike, my life
A series of dips and ridges,
Happiness a free-wheeling
Past fragrant hawthorn hedges.

Cape and sou'wester streamed
With rain as I rode to school
Side-tracking the bus routes.
Night after night I dreamed
Of valves, pumps, sprockets,
Reflectors and repair kits.

Soon there were long rides
In the country, wet weekends
Playing cards in the kitchens
Of mountain youth hostels,
Day-runs to Monaghan,
Rough and exotic roads.

It went with me to Dublin
Where I sold it the same winter;
But its wheels still sing
In the memory, stars that turn
About an eternal centre,
The bright spokes glittering.

Going Home

(for John Hewitt)

I am taking leave of the trees,
The beech, the cedar, the elm,
The mild woods of these parts
Misted with car exhaust
And sawdust, and the last
Gasps of the poisoned nymphs.

I have watched girls walking
And children playing under
Lilac and rhododendron,
And me flicking my ash
Into the rose bushes
As if I owned the place;

As if the trees responded
To my ignorant admiration
Before dawn when the branches
Glitter at first light,
Or later when the finches
Disappear for the night;

And often thought if I lived
Long enough in this house
I would turn into a tree
Like somebody in Ovid
— A small tree certainly
But a tree nevertheless —

Perhaps befriend the oak,
The chestnut and the yew,
Become a home for birds,
A shelter for the nymphs,
And gaze out over the downs
As if I belonged here too.

But where I am going the trees
Are few and far between —
No richly forested slopes,
Not for a long time,
And few winking woodlands.
There are no nymphs to be seen.

Out there you would look in vain
For a rose-bush; but find,
Rooted in stony ground,
A last stubborn growth
Battered by constant rain
And twisted by the sea wind

With nothing to recommend it
But its harsh tenacity
Between the blinding windows
And the forests of the sea,
As if its very existence
Were a reason to continue.

Crone, crow, scarecrow,
Its worn fingers scrabbling
At a torn sky, it stands
On the edge of everything
Like a burnt-out angel
Raising petitionary hands.

Grotesque by day, at twilight
An almost tragic figure
Of anguish and despair,
It merges into the funeral
Cloud-continent of night
As if it belongs there.

The Chinese Restaurant in Portrush

Before the first visitor comes the spring
Softening the sharp air of the coast
In time for the first seasonal 'invasion'.
Today the place is as it might have been,
Gentle and almost hospitable. A girl
Strides past the Northern Counties Hotel,
Light-footed, swinging a book bag,
And the doors that were shut all winter
Against the north wind and the sea mist
Lie open to the street, where one
By one the gulls go window-shopping
And an old wolfhound dozes in the sun.

While I sit with my paper and prawn chow mein
Under a framed photograph of Hong Kong
The proprietor of the Chinese restaurant
Stands at the door as if the world were young,
Watching the first yacht hoist a sail
— An ideogram on sea-cloud — and the light
Of heaven upon the hills of Donegal;
And whistles a little tune, dreaming of home.

Camus in Ulster

Deprived though we were of your climatic privileges
And raised in a northern land of rain and haze
We too knew the cherished foe, the blaze
Of headlights on a coast road, the cicadas
Chattering like watches in our sodden hedges;
Yet never imagined the plague to come,
So long had it slept there in the mind —
The police charge and the stricken home,
An old blues number playing to the plague wind.

North Wind

I shall never forget the wind
On this benighted coast.
It works itself into the mind
Like the high keen of a lost
Lear-spirit in agony
Condemned for eternity

To wander cliff and cove
Without comfort, without love.
It whistles off the stars
And the existential, stark
Face of the cosmic dark.
We crouch to roaring fires.

Yet there are mornings when,
Even in midwinter, sunlight
Flares, and a rare stillness
Lies upon roof and garden —
Each object eldritch-bright,
The sea scarred but at peace.

Then, from the ship we say
Is the lit town where we live
(Our whiskey-and-forecast world),
A smaller ship that sheltered
All night in the restless bay
Will weigh anchor and leave.

What did they think of us
During their brief sojourn?
A string of lights on the prom
Dancing mad in the storm —
Who lives in such a place?
And will they ever return?

The shops open at nine
As they have always done,
The wrapped-up bourgeoisie
Hardened by wind and sea.
The newspapers are late
But the milk shines in its crate.

Everything swept so clean
By tempest, wind and rain!
Elated, you might believe
That this was the first day —
A false sense of reprieve,
For the climate is here to stay.

So best prepare for the worst
That chaos and old night
Can do to us: were we not
Raised on such expectations,
Our hearts starred with frost
Through many generations?

Elsewhere the olive grove,
Naked lunch on the grass,
Poppies and parasols,
Blue skies and mythic love.
Here only the stricken souls
No springtime can release.

Prospero and his people never
Came to these stormy parts;
Few do who have the choice.
Yet, blasting the subtler arts,
That weird, plaintive voice
Sings now and for ever.

Portrush

Greta

The old motorbike she was
The first woman in those
Parts to ride — a noble
Norton — disintegrates
With rusty iron gates
In some abandoned stable;

But lives in sepia shades
Where an emancipated
Country schoolteacher
Of nineteen thirty-eight
Smiles from her frame before
Broaching the mountain roads.

Forty years later she
Shakes slack on the fire
To douse it while she goes
Into Bushmills to buy
Groceries and newspaper
And exchange courtesies.

Then back to a pot of tea
And the early-evening news
(Some fresh atrocity);
Washes up to the sound
Of a chat show, one phrase
Of Bach going round and round

In her head as she stares
Out at the wintry moon
And thinks of her daughters
So very far away —
Although the telephone
Makes nonsense of that today.

Out there beyond the edge
Of the golf course tosses
The ghost of the *Girona*,
Flagship of the Armada —
History; does the knowledge
Alter the world she sees?

Or do her thoughts travel
By preference among
Memories of her naval
Husband, thirty years
Drowned, the watercolours
And instruments unstrung?

A tentatively romantic
Figure once, she became
Merely an old lady like
Many another, with
Her favourite programme
And her sustaining faith.

She sits now and watches
Incredulously as some mad
Whippersnapper howls
His love song and the gulls
Snuggle down on the beaches,
The rooks in the churchyard.

'Songs of Praise'

Tonight, their simple church grown glamorous,
The proud parishioners of the outlying parts
Lift up their hymn books and their hearts
To please the outside-broadcast cameras.
The darkness deepens; day draws to a close;
A well-bred sixth-former yawns with her nose.

Outside, the hymn dies among rocks and dunes.
Conflicting rhythms of the incurious sea,
Not even contemptuous of these tiny tunes,
Take over where our thin ascriptions fail.
Down there the silence of the laboratory,
Trombone dispatches of the beleaguered whale.

Courtyards in Delft

— Pieter de Hooch, 1659

(for Gordon Woods)

Oblique light on the trite, on brick and tile —
Immaculate masonry, and everywhere that
Water tap, that broom and wooden pail
To keep it so. House-proud, the wives
Of artisans pursue their thrifty lives
Among scrubbed yards, modest but adequate.
Foliage is sparse, and clings; no breeze
Ruffles the trim composure of those trees.

No spinet-playing emblematic of
The harmonies and disharmonies of love,
No lewd fish, no fruit, no wide-eyed bird
About to fly its cage while a virgin
Listens to her seducer, mars the chaste
Perfection of the thing and the thing made.
Nothing is random, nothing goes to waste.
We miss the dirty dog, the fiery gin.

That girl with her back to us who waits
For her man to come home for his tea
Will wait till the paint disintegrates
And ruined dikes admit the esurient sea;
Yet this is life too, and the cracked
Outhouse door a verifiable fact
As vividly mnemonic as the sunlit
Railings that front the houses opposite.

I lived there as a boy and know the coal
Glittering in its shed, late-afternoon
Lambency informing the deal table,
The ceiling cradled in a radiant spoon.

I must be lying low in a room there,
A strange child with a taste for verse,
While my hard-nosed companions dream of war
On parched veldt and fields of rainswept gorse.

Rathlin

A long time since the last scream cut short —
Then an unnatural silence; and then
A natural silence, slowly broken
By the shearwater, by the sporadic
Conversation of crickets, the bleak
Reminder of a metaphysical wind.
Ages of this, till the report
Of an outboard motor at the pier
Shatters the dream-time and we land
As if we were the first visitors here.

The whole island a sanctuary where amazed
Oneiric species whistle and chatter,
Evacuating rock-face and cliff-top.
Cerulean distance, an oceanic haze —
Nothing but sea-smoke to the ice-cap
And the odd somnolent freighter.
Bombs doze in the housing estates
But here they are through with history —
Custodians of a lone light which repeats
One simple statement to the turbulent sea.

A long time since the unspeakable violence —
Since Somhairle Buí, powerless on the mainland,
Heard the screams of the Rathlin women
Born, seconds later, on a north-east wind.
Only the cry of the shearwater
And the roar of the outboard motor
Disturb the singular peace. Spray-blind,
We leave here the infancy of the race,
Unsure among the pitching surfaces
Whether the future lies before us or behind.

Derry Morning

The mist clears and the cavities
Glow black in the rubbled city's
Broken mouth. An early crone,
Muse of a fitful revolution
Wasted by the fray, she sees
Her *aisling* falter in the breeze,
Her oak-grove vision hesitate
By empty dock and city gate.

Here it began, and here at last
It fades into the finite past
Or seems to: clattering shadows whop
Mechanically over pub and shop.
A strangely pastoral silence rules
The shining roofs and murmuring schools;
For this is how the centuries work —
Two steps forward, one step back.

Hard to believe this tranquil place,
Its desolation almost peace,
Was recently a boom-town wild
With expectation, each unscheduled
Incident a measurable
Tremor on the Richter scale
Of world events, each vibrant scene
Translated to the drizzling screen.

What of the change envisioned here,
The quantum leap from fear to fire?
Smoke from a thousand chimneys strains
One way beneath the returning rains
That shroud the bomb-sites, while the fog
Of time receives the ideologue.
A Russian freighter bound for home
Mourns to the city in its gloom.

Rock Music

The ocean glittered quietly in the moonlight
While heavy metal rocked the discotheques;
Space-age Hondas gurgled half the night,
Fired by the prospect of fortuitous sex.
I sat late at the window, blind with rage,
And listened to the tumult down below,
Trying to concentrate on the printed page
As if such obsolete bumph could save us now.

(Frank Ifield, Helen Shapiro, where are you now?
Every night by the window here I sit.
Sandie and Bobby, I still remember you —
As for the Arcadia, though I remember it,
It no longer remembers the uncouth Coke-heads
Who trembled here in nineteen fifty-six
In ice-cream parlours and amusement arcades;
Oddities all, we knew none of the tricks.

Cinema organ, easy listening, swing, doowop, bebop,
Sedate me with your subliminal sublime
And give me that old trashy fifties pop,
Suburban burblings of an earlier time;
The boogie bins bouncing in rotary light,
Give me my toxic shame, mean woman blues,
That old self-pity where, lonesome tonight,
I sit here snarling in my blue suede shoes.)

Next morning, wandering on the strand, I heard
Left-over echoes of the night before
Dwindle to echoes, and a single bird
Drown with a whistle that residual roar.
Rock music started up on every side —
Whisper of algae, click of stone on stone,
A thousand limpets left by the ebb tide
Unanimous in their silent inquisition.

A Blackbird

One morning in the month of June
I was coming out of this door
And found myself in a garden,
A sanctuary of light and air
Transplanted from the Hesperides,
No sound of machinery anywhere,
When from a bramble bush a hidden
Blackbird suddenly gave tongue,
Its diffident, resilient song
Breaking the silence of the seas.

The Attic

(for John and Evelyn Montague)

Under the night window
    A dockyard fluorescence,
Muse-light on the city,
    A world of heightened sense.

At work in your attic
    Up here under the roof —
Listen, can you hear me
    Turning over a new leaf?

Silent by ticking lamplight
    I stare at the blank spaces,
Reflecting the composure
    Of patient surfaces —

I who know nothing
    Scribbling on the off-chance,
Darkening the white page,
    Cultivating my ignorance.

The Old Snaps

I keep your old snaps in the bottom drawer —
The icons of a more than personal love.
Look, three sisters out of Chekhov
('When will we ever go to Moscow?')
Ranged on the steps of the schoolhouse
Where their mother is head teacher,
Out on the rocks, or holding down their hair
In a high wind on a North Antrim shore.

Later, yourself alone among sand-hills
Striking a slightly fictional pose,
Life-ready and impervious to harm
In your wind-blown school uniform,
While the salt sea air fills
Your young body with ozone
And fine sand trickles into your shoes.
I think I must have known you even then.

We 'went to Moscow', and we will again.
Meanwhile we walk on the strand
And smile as if for the first time
While the children play in the sand.
We have never known a worse winter
But the old snaps are always there,
Framed for ever in your heart and mine
Where no malicious hands can twist or tear.

Everything Is Going to Be All Right

How should I not be glad to contemplate
the clouds clearing beyond the dormer window
and a high tide reflected on the ceiling?
There will be dying, there will be dying,
but there is no need to go into that.
The lines flow from the hand unbidden
and the hidden source is the watchful heart;
the sun rises in spite of everything
and the far cities are beautiful and bright.
I lie here in a riot of sunlight
watching the day break and the clouds flying.
Everything is going to be all right.

Heraclitus on Rivers

Nobody steps into the same river twice.
The same river is never the same
Because that is the nature of water.
Similarly your changing metabolism
Means that you are no longer you.
The cells die, and the precise
Configuration of the heavenly bodies
When she told you she loved you
Will not come again in this lifetime.

You will tell me that you have executed
A monument more lasting than bronze;
But even bronze is perishable.
Your best poem, you know the one I mean,
The very language in which the poem
Was written, and the idea of language,
All these things will pass away in time.

The Sea in Winter

(for Desmond O'Grady)

Desmond, what of the blue nights,
the ultramarines and violets
of your white island in the south,
'far-shining star of dark-blue Earth',
and the boat-lights in the tiny port
where we drank so much retsina?
Up here where the air is thinner,
in a draughty bungalow in Portstewart

beside my 'distant northern sea',
I imagine a moon of Asia Minor
bright on your nightly industry.
Sometimes, rounding the cliff top
at dusk, under the convent wall,
and finding the little town lit up
as if for some island festival,
I pretend not to be here at all;

that the shopfronts along the prom,
whose fluorescence blinds the foam
and shingle, are the dancing lights
of Náousa — those gregarious nights! —
that these frosty pavements are
the pavements of that distant star;
that the cold, glistening sea mist
eclipses Naxos to the east.

But morning scatters down the strand
relics of last night's gale-force wind;
far out, the Atlantic faintly breaks,
seaweed exhales among the rocks
and fretfully the spent winds fan
the cenotaph and the lifeboat mine;
from door to door the Ormo van
delivers, while the stars decline.

Portstewart, Portrush, Portballintrae —
un beau pays mal habité,
policed by rednecks in dark cloth
and roving gangs of tartan youth.
No place for a gentleman like you.
The good, the beautiful and the true
have a tough time of it; and yet
there *is* that Hebridean sunset,

and a strange poetry of decay
charms the condemned hotels by day,
while in the dark hours the rattle
of a cat knocking over a milk-bottle
on a distant doorstep by moonlight
can set you thinking half the night.
The moon of Nineveh and Tyre
shines still on the Harbour Bar.

You too know the delirious sense
of working on the circumference —
the midnight oil, familiar sea,
elusive dawn epiphany,
faith that the trivia doodled here
will bear their fruit sometime, somewhere;
that the long winter months may bring
gifts to the goddess in the spring.

The sea in winter, where she walks,
vents its displeasure on the rocks.
The something rotten in the state
infects the innocent; the spite
mankind has brought to this infernal
backwater destroys the soul;
it sneaks into the daily life,
sunders the husband from the wife.

But let me never forget the weird
facticity of this strange seaboard,
the heroism and cowardice
of living on the edge of space,
or ever again contemptuously
refuse its plight; for history
ignores those who ignore it, not
the ignorant whom it begot.

To start from scratch, to make it new,
forsake the grey skies for the blue,
to find the narrow road to the deep
north the road to Damascus, leap
before we look! The ideal future
shines out of our better nature,
dimly visible from afar:
'The sun is but a morning star.'

One day, the day each one conceives —
the day the Dying Gaul revives,
the day the girl among the trees
strides through our wrecked technologies,
the stones speak out, the rainbow ends,
the wine goes round among the friends,
the lost are found, the parted lovers
lie at peace beneath the covers.

Meanwhile the given life goes on;
there is nothing new under the sun.
The dogs bark and the caravan
glides mildly by; and if the dawn
that wakes us now should also find us
cured of our ancient colour-blindness . . .
I who know nothing go to teach
while a new day crawls up the beach.

Hunger

(for Paul Durcan)

While a late thaw began in the boarded eaves
I left, exhausted, that city nobody leaves
Without being marked by it; signed on
For Newcastle-upon-Tyne and so to Spain,
Renouncing the tightly corseted lives,
The many windows flashing in the sun.
Dream on, dream homes, until I come again!

Later the wives and the hard-earned estate,
The admiration of the acknowledged great;
But who could hope wholly to sublimate
The bad years, the imperious gratitude
Working like hunger at the very bone?
And so, my larder dim with surplus food,
My polished windows blazing in the sun,

Waking these days I sometimes think myself
Back in that attic with its empty shelf.
Strangely enough, it was enormous fun
Glaring, a madman, into the bap faces
Of outraged butchers and policemen
And acting the idiot in public places.
The conquering soul betrayed a manic grin.

Born of the earth, I made terms with the earth,
This being the only thing of lasting worth.
Beside my bed the dog-eared gods of art
Made way for fragrant works on crop rotation,
The agriculture where all cultures start.
The typewriter fell silent; rod and gun
Went out with me to prowl the watchful dawn.

Yes, I shook hands with Hitler; knew disgrace.
But time heals everything; I rose again.
Now I can look my butcher in the face.
Besides, did I not once, as a young man,
Cure myself of incipient tuberculosis
Inhaling four sub-zero nights and days
Perched on the screaming roof of a freight train?

One fortunate in both would have us choose
'Perfection of the life or of the work'.
Nonsense, you work best on a full stomach
As everybody over thirty knows —
For who, unbreakfasted, will love the lark?
Prepare your protein-fed epiphanies,
Your heavenly mansions blazing in the dark.

Tractatus

'The world is everything that is the case'
From the fly giving up in the coal-shed
To the Winged Victory of Samothrace.
Give blame, praise, to the fumbling God
Who hides, shame-facèdly, His agèd face;
Whose light retires behind its veil of cloud.

The world, though, is also so much more —
Everything that is the case imaginatively.
Tacitus believed mariners could *hear*
The sun sinking into the western sea;
And who would question that titanic roar,
The steam rising wherever the edge may be?

The Andean Flute

He dances to that music in the wood
As if history were no more than a dream.
Who said the banished gods were gone for good?

The furious rhythm creates a manic mood,
Piercing the twilight like a mountain stream.
He dances to that music in the wood.

We might have put on Bach or Buxtehude,
But a chance impulse chose the primal scream.
Who said the banished gods were gone for good?

An Inca frenzy fires his northern blood.
His child-heart picking up the tribal beam,
He dances to that music in the wood.

A puff of snow bursts where the birches brood;
Along the lane the earliest snowdrops gleam.
Who said the banished gods were gone for good?

It is the ancient cry for warmth and food
That moves him. Acting out an ancient theme,
He dances to that music in the wood.
Who said the banished gods were gone for good?

The Dawn Chorus

It is not sleep itself but dreams we miss,
Say the psychologists; and the poets too.
We yearn for that reality in this.

There is another world resides in this,
Amidst the muddy fields a pool of blue.
It is not sleep itself but dreams we miss.

If we could once achieve a synthesis
Of the archaic and the entirely new . . .
We yearn for that reality in this.

But, wide awake, clear-eyed with cowardice,
The flaming seraphim we find untrue.
It is not sleep itself but dreams we miss.

Listening heartbroken to the dawn chorus,
Clutching the certainty that once we flew,
We yearn for that reality in this.

Awaiting still our metamorphosis,
We hoard the fragments of what once we knew.
It is not sleep itself but dreams we miss.
We yearn for that reality in this.

Katie at the Pool

My four-year-old daughter
points up at the low
ceiling with a cry:
'Look at the shadow
of the water on the sky!'

Radio Days

(*for John Scotney*)

The silence of the ether . . .
What can be going on
In the art-deco liner?

Ah, now the measured pips,
A stealth of strings
Tickling the fretwork throat,

Woodwinds entering
Delicately, the clarinet
Ascending to a lark-like note.

Seven o'clock —
News time, and the merciful
Voice of Tom Crowe

Explains with sorrow
That the world we know
Is coming to an end.

Even as he speaks
We can hear furniture
Creak and slide on the decks.

But first a brief recital
Of resonant names —
Mozart, Schubert, Brahms.

The sun shines,
And a new day begins
To the strains of a horn concerto.

The Drawing Board

You think I am your servant but you are wrong —
The service lies with you. During your long
Labours at me, I am the indulgent wood,
Tolerant of your painstaking ineptitude.
Your poems were torn from me by violence;
I am here to receive your homage in dark silence.

Remembering the chainsaw surgery and the seaward groan,
Like a bound and goaded exodus from Babylon,
I pray for a wood spirit to make me dance,
To scare your pants off and upset your balance,
Destroy the sedate poise with which you pour
Forth your ephemeral stream of literature.

When I was a pine and lived in a cold climate
I listened to leaf rumours about our fate;
But I have come a long way since then
To watch the sun glint on your reflective pen.
The hurt I do resent, and my consolation
Will be the unspoilt paper when you have gone.

And yet I love you, even in your ignorance,
Perhaps because at last you are making sense —
Talking to me, not through me, recognizing
That it is I alone who let you sing
Wood music; hitherto shadowy and dumb,
I speak to you now as your indispensable medium.

Sunday Morning

We wake and watch the sun make bright
The corners of our London flat —
No sound but the sporadic, surly
Snarl of a car making an early
Dash for the country or the coast.
This is the time I like the most
When, for an hour or two, the strife
And strain of the late bourgeois life

Let up, we lie and grin to hear
The children bickering next door —
Hilarious formulations based
On a weird logic we have lost.
Oil crises and vociferous crowds
Seem as far off as tiny clouds;
The long-range forecast prophesies
Mean temperatures and azure skies.

Out in the park where Celia's father
Died, the Sunday people gather —
Residents towed by Afghan hounds,
Rastafarians trailing 'sounds',
Provincial tourists, Japanese
Economists, Saudi families,
Fresh-faced American college kids
Making out in the green shades.

A chiliastic prick, I prowl
Among the dog-lovers and growl,
Among the kite-fliers and fly
The private kite of poetry —
A sort of winged sandwich board
El-Grecoed to receive the word;
An airborne, tremulous brochure
Proclaiming that the end is near.

Black diplomats with gorgeous wives,
Promenading, notice the natives
Dozing beside the palace gates —
Old ladies under wide straw hats
Who can remember *Chu Chin Chow*
And Kitchener. Exhausted now
By decades of retrenchment, they
Wait for the rain at close of play.

Asia now for a thousand years —
A flower that blooms and disappears
In a sandstorm; every artifact
A pure, self-referential act,
That the intolerant soul may be
Retrieved from triviality
And the locked heart, so long in pawn
To steel, redeemed by flesh and bone.

One of these Nights

(*for Fleur Fitzgerald*)

A pregnant moon of August
Composes the rooftops'
Unventilated slopes;
Dispenses to the dust
Its milky balm. A blue
Buzzard blinks in the zoo.

Cashel and Angkor Wat
Are not more ghostly than
London now, its squares
Bone-pale in the moonlight,
Its quiet thoroughfares
A sea of desolation.

The grime of an ephemeral
Culture is swept clean
By that celestial hoover,
The refuse of an era
Consumed like polythene
In its impartial glare.

A train trembles deep
In the earth; vagrants sleep
Beside the revolving doors
Of vast department stores
Past whose alarm systems
The moonlight blandly streams.

A breeze-ruffled news-stand
Headlines the dole queues,
The bleak no-longer-news
Of racism and inflation —
Straws in the rising wind
That heralds the cyclone.

It all happened before —
The road to Wigan Pier,
The long road from Jarrow
To the tea room at the Ritz;
Munich, the Phoney War,
The convoys and the Blitz.

One of these nights quiescent
Sirens will start to go
— A dog howl reminiscent
Of forty years ago —
And sleepy people file
Down to the shelters while

Radiant warplanes come
Droning up the Thames from
Gravesend to Blackfriars,
Westminster and Mayfair,
Their incandescent flowers
Unfolding everywhere.

Enchanted foliage, bright
Water as in an old film
In sumptuous black and white
— This is the true realm,
The real earth before
Business and empire;
And life begins tonight.

A Garage in Co. Cork

Surely you paused at this roadside oasis
In your nomadic youth, and saw the mound
Of never-used cement, the curious faces,
The soft-drink ads and the uneven ground
Rainbowed with oily puddles, where a snail
Had scrawled its pearly, phosphorescent trail.

Like a frontier store-front in an old western
It might have nothing behind it but thin air,
Building materials, fruit boxes, scrap iron,
Dust-laden shrubs and coils of rusty wire,
A cabbage white fluttering in the sodden
Silence of an untended kitchen garden —

Nirvana! But the cracked panes reveal a dark
Interior echoing with the cries of children.
Here in this quiet corner of Co. Cork
A family ate, slept, and watched the rain
Dance clean and cobalt the exhausted grit
So that the mind shrank from the glare of it.

Where did they go? South Boston? Cricklewood?
Somebody somewhere thinks of this as home,
Remembering the old pumps where they stood,
Antique now, squirting juice into a cream
Lagonda or a dung-caked tractor while
A cloud swam on a cloud-reflecting tile.

Surely a whitewashed suntrap at the back
Gave way to hens, wild thyme, and the first few
Shadowy yards of an overgrown cart track,
Tyres in the branches such as Noah knew —
Beyond, a swoop of mountain where you heard,
Disconsolate in the haze, a single blackbird.

Left to itself, the functional will cast
A deathbed glow of picturesque abandon.
The intact antiquities of the recent past,
Dropped from the retail catalogues, return
To the materials that gave rise to them
And shine with a late sacramental gleam.

A god who spent the night here once rewarded
Natural courtesy with eternal life —
Changing to petrol pumps, that they be spared
For ever there, an old man and his wife.
The virgin who escaped his dark design
Sanctions the townland from her prickly shrine.

We might be anywhere but are in one place only,
One of the milestones of Earth residence
Unique in each particular, the thinly
Peopled hinterland serenely tense —
Not in the hope of a resplendent future
But with a sure sense of its intrinsic nature.

The Woods

Two years we spent
down there, in a quaint
outbuilding bright with recent paint.

A green retreat,
secluded and sedate,
part of a once great estate,

it watched our old
banger as it growled
with guests and groceries through heat and cold,

and heard you tocsin
mealtimes with a spoon
while I sat typing in the sun.

Above the yard
an old clock had expired
the night Lenin arrived in Petrograd.

Hapsburgs and Romanovs
had removed their gloves
in the drawing-rooms and alcoves

of the manor house;
but these illustrious
ghosts never imposed on us.

Enough that the pond
steamed, the apples ripened,
the chestnuts on the gravel opened.

Ragwort and hemlock,
cinquefoil and ladysmock
throve in the shadows at the back;

beneath the trees
foxgloves and wood anemones
looked up with tearful metamorphic eyes.

We woke the rooks
on narrow, winding walks
familiar from the story books,

or visited
a disused garden shed
where gas masks from the war decayed;

and we knew peace
splintering the thin ice
on the bathtub drinking trough for cows.

But how could we
survive indefinitely
so far from the city and the sea?

Finding, at last,
too creamy for our taste
the fat profusion of that feast,

we carried on
to chaos and confusion,
our birthright and our proper portion.

Another light
than ours convenes the mute
attention of those woods tonight —

while we, released
from that pale paradise,
confront the darkness in another place.

Craigvara House

That was the year
of the black nights and clear
mornings, a mild elation touched with fear;

a watchful anomie,
heart silence, day-long reverie
while the wind made harpstrings on the sea

and the first
rain of winter burst
earthwards as if quenching a great thirst.

A mist of spray
hung over the shore all day
while I slumped there re-reading *La Nausée*

or knocked a coal,
releasing squeaky gas until
it broke and tumbled into its hot hole.

Night fell on a rough
sea, on a moonlit basalt cliff,
huts with commandments painted on the roof,

and rain wept down
the raw slates of the town,
cackling maniacally in pipe and drain.

I slowly came
to treasure my asylum
(a flat with a sea view, the living-room

furnished with frayed
chintz, cane chairs and faded
watercolours of Slemish and Torr Head —

no phone, no television,
nothing to break my concentration,
the new-won knowledge of my situation);

and it was there,
choosing my words with care,
I sat down and began to write once more.

When snowflakes
wandered on to the rocks
I thought, home is where the heart breaks —

the lost domain
of weekends in the rain,
the Sunday sundae and the sexual pain.

I stared each night
at a glow of yellow light
over the water where the interned sat tight

and during storms
imagined the clenched farms
'with dreadful faces throng'd and fiery arms'.

Sometime before
spring I found in there
the frequency I had been looking for

and crossed by night
a dark channel, my eyesight
focused upon a flickering pier-light.

I slept then and,
waking early, listened
entranced to the pea-whistle sound

of a first thrush
practising on a whin bush
a new air picked up in Marrakesh.

And then your car
parked with a known roar
and you stood smiling at the door —

as if we might
consider a bad night
as over and step out into the sunlight.

The Terminal Bar

(for Philip Haas)

The television set hung
in its wire-net cage,
protected from the flung
bottles of casual rage,
is fetish and icon
providing all we want
of magic and redemption,
routine and sentiment.
The year-old tinsels hang
where an unclaimed no-hoper
trembles; fly-corpses cling
to the grimy flypaper.
Manhattan snows swarm
on star-boxed waters,
steam trails from warm
subway ventilators . . .
Welcome to the planet,
its fluorescent beers
buzzing in the desolate
silence of the spheres.
Slam the door and knock
the snow from your shoe,
admit that the vast dark
at last defeated you.
Nobody found the Grail
or conquered outer space;
join the clientele
watching itself increase.

The Globe in Carolina

The earth spins to my fingertips and
Pauses beneath my outstretched hand;
White water seethes against the green
Capes where the continents begin.
Warm breezes move the pines and stir
The hot dust of the piedmont where
Night glides inland from town to town.
I love to see that sun go down.

It sets in a coniferous haze
Beyond Georgia while the anglepoise
Rears like a moon to shed its savage
Radiance on the desolate page,
On Dvořàk sleeves and Audubon
Bird-prints; an electronic brain
Records the concrete music of
Our hardware in the heavens above.

From Hatteras to the Blue Ridge
Night spreads like ink on the unhedged
Tobacco fields and clucking lakes,
Bringing the lights on in the rocks
And swamps, the farms and motor courts,
Substantial cities, kitsch resorts —
Until, to the mild theoptic eye,
America is its own night-sky.

Out in the void and staring hard
At the dim stone where we were reared,
Great mother, now the gods have gone
We place our faith in you alone,
Inverting the procedures which
Knelt us to things beyond our reach.
Drop of the ocean, may your salt
Astringency redeem our fault.

Veined marble, if we only knew,
In practice as in theory, true
Redemption lies not in the thrust
Of action only, but the trust
We place in our peripheral
Night garden in the glory hole
Of space, a home from home, and what
Devotion we can bring to it.

You lie, an ocean to the east,
Your limbs composed, your mind at rest,
Asleep in a sunrise which will be
Your midday when it reaches me;
And what misgivings I might have
About the final value of
Our humanism pale before
The mere fact of your being there.

Five miles away a southbound freight
Sings its euphoria to the state
And passes on; unfinished work
Awaits me in the scented dark.
The halved globe, slowly turning, hugs
Its silence, while the lightning bugs
Are quiet beneath the open window,
Listening to that lonesome whistle blow.

Squince

The eyes are clouded where
　　He lies in a veined dish.
Is this the salmon of knowledge
　　Or merely a dead fish?

A forest of symbols here —
　　Swan, heron, goat,
Druidic stone circle, fuchsia-
　　Buried hill fort;

And the village is of clear-cut
　　Resonant artifacts:
A pink-washed grocery shop,
　　A yellow *telefón* box.

We live now in a future
　　Prehistory, the ancient
Mystery surviving in
　　The power to enchant

Of the sun going down
　　In a thicket of hazel trees
While ferns at the window
　　Nod in the everbreeze.

Mount Gabriel

As if planted there by giant golfers in the skies,
White in the gloaming, last before New Brunswick,
The geodesic domes have left their caves
To sit out in the summer sunset. Angels
Beamed at Namancos and Bayona, sick
With exile, they yearn homeward now, their eyes
Tuned to the ultramarine, first-star-pierced dark
Reflected on the dark, incoming waves —
Who, aliens, burnt-out meteorites, time capsules,
Are here for ever now as intermediaries
Between the big bang and our scattered souls.

The Hunt by Night

— Uccello, 1465

Flickering shades,
   stick figures, lithe game,
swift flights of bison in a cave
where man the maker killed to live;
   but neolithic bush became
     the midnight woods

   of nursery walls,
     the ancient fears mutated
to play, horses to rocking-horses
tamed and framed to courtly uses,
   crazed no more by foetid
     bestial howls

   but rampant to
     the pageantry they share
and echoes of the hunting horn
at once peremptory and forlorn.
   The mild herbaceous air
     is lemon-blue,

   the glade aglow
     with pleasant mysteries,
diuretic depots, pungent prey;
and midnight hints at break of day
   where, among sombre trees,
     the greyhounds go

   wild with suspense
     leaping to left and right,
their cries receding to a point
masked by obscurities of paint
   as if our hunt by night,
     so very tense,

so long pursued,
in what dark cave begun
and not yet done, were not the great
adventure we suppose but some elaborate
spectacle put on for fun
and not for food.

Girls on the Bridge

— Munch, 1901

Audible trout,
notional midges. Beds,
lamplight and crisp linen wait
in the house there for the sedate
limbs and averted heads
of the girls out

late on the bridge.
The dusty road that slopes
past is perhaps the high road south,
a symbol of world-wondering youth,
of adolescent hopes
and privileges;

but stops to find
the girls content to gaze
at the unplumbed, reflective lake,
their plangent conversational quack
expressive of calm days
and peace of mind.

Grave daughters
of time, you lightly toss
your hair as the long shadows grow
and night begins to fall. Although
your laughter calls across
the dark waters,

a ghastly sun
watches in pale dismay.
Oh you may laugh, being as you are
fair sisters of the evening star,
but wait — if not today
a day will dawn

when the bad dreams
you scarcely know will scatter
the punctual increment of your lives.
The road resumes, and where it curves,
a mile from where you chatter,
somebody screams.

Brighton Beach

(for Paul Smyth)

I

Remember those awful parties
In dreary Belfast flats,
The rough sectarian banter
In Lavery's back bar,
The boisterous takeaways
And moonlight on wet slates?

Remember the place you rented
At the end of a muddy lane
Somewhere near Muckamore?
No light, so in midwinter
You slept in the afternoon
And lay there until dawn.

Remember the time we drove
To Donegal and you talked
For hours to fishermen
You had worked with while I,
Out of my depths in those
Waters, loafed on the quays?

Now, pushing forty, we roam
At ease along the prom,
Life-buffeted to be sure
But grown sober and wise.
The sea shuffles ashore
Beneath pale mackerel skies.

2

From the far end of the pier
I imagine the sun-gleam
On a thousand *deux-chevaux*.
Over there they explore
Balbec and sip Pernod
In a Monet-monoxide dream.

Europe thrives, but the offshore
Islanders year by year
Decline, the spirit of empire
Fugitive as always.
Now, in this rancorous peace,
Should come the spirit of place.

Too late though, for already
Places as such are dead
Or nearly; the loved sea
Reflects banality.
Not so in the old days
The retired sailor says.

But the faded Georgian bricks
Towering over the shore
Remain, like the upright
Old men with walking sticks
Out for a last stroll before
Turning in for the night.

Beyond the Pale

I lie and imagine a first light gleam in the bay
    After one more night of erosion and nearer the grave,
Then stand and gaze from the window at break of day
    As a shearwater skims the ridge of an incoming wave;
And I think of my son a dolphin in the Aegean,
    A sprite among sails knife-bright in a seasonal wind,
And wish he were here where currachs walk on the ocean
    To ease with his talk the solitude locked in my mind.

I sit on a stone after noon and consider the glow
    Of the sun through mist, a pearl bulb containèdly fierce;
A rain shower darkens the schist for a minute or so,
    Then it drifts away and the sloe-black patches disperse.
Croagh Patrick towers like Naxos over the water
    And I think of my daughter at work on her difficult art
And wish she were with me now between thrush and plover,
    Wild thyme and sea-thrift, to lift the weight from my heart.

The young sit smoking and laughing on the bridge at evening
    Like birds on a telephone pole or notes on a score.
A tin whistle squeals in the parlour, once more it is raining,
    Turfsmoke inclines and a wind whines under the door;
And I lie and imagine the lights going on in the harbour
    Of white-housed Náousa, your clear definition at night,
And wish you were here to upstage my disconsolate labour
    As I glance through a few thin pages and switch off the light.

Ovid in Tomis

What coarse god
Was the gearbox in the rain
Beside the road?

What nereid the unsinkable
Coca-Cola
Knocking the icy rocks?

They stare me out
With the chaste gravity
And feral pride

Of noble savages
Set down
On an alien shore.

It is so long
Since my own transformation
Into a stone,

I often forget
That there was a time
Before my name

Was mud in the mouths
Of the Danube,
A dirty word in Rome.

Imagine Byron banished
To Botany Bay
Or Wilde to Dawson City

And you have some idea
How it is for me
On the shores of the Black Sea.

I who once strode
Head-high in the forum,
A living legend,

Fasten my sheepskin
By greasy waters
In a Scythian wind.

My wife and friends
Do what they can
On my behalf;

Though from Tiberius,
Whom God preserve,
I expect nothing.

But I don't want
To die here
In the back of beyond

Among these morose
Dice-throwing Getes
And the dust of Thrace.

No doubt in time
To come this huddle of
Mud huts will be

A handsome city,
An important port,
A popular resort

With an oil pipeline,
Smart terraces
And even a dignified

Statue of Ovid
Gazing out to sea
From the promenade;

But for the moment
It is merely a place
Where I have to be.

Six years now
Since my relegation
To this town

By the late Augustus.
The *Halieutica*,
However desultory,

Gives me a sense
Of purpose,
However factitious;

But I think it's the birds
That please me most,
The cranes and pelicans.

I often sit in the dunes
Listening hard
To the uninhibited

Virtuosity of a lark
Serenading the sun
And meditate upon

The transience
Of earthly dominion,
The perfidy of princes.

Mediocrity, they say,
Consoles itself
With the reflection

That genius so often
Comes to a bad end.
The things adversity

Teaches us
About human nature
As the aphorisms strike home!

I know the simple life
Would be right for me
If I were a simple man.

I have a real sense
Of the dumb spirit
In boulder and tree;

Skimming stones, I wince
With vicarious pain
As a slim quoit goes in.

And the six-foot reeds
Of the delta,
The pathos there!

Whenever they bend
And sigh in the wind
It is not merely Syrinx

Remembering Syrinx
But Syrinx keening
Her naked terror

Of the certain future,
She and her kind
Being bulk-destined

For pulping machines
And the cording
Of motor-car tyres.

Pan is dead, and already
I feel an ancient
Unity leave the earth,

The bowl avoid my eye
As if ashamed
Of my failure to keep faith.

(It knows that I
Have exchanged belief
For documentation.)

The Muse is somewhere
Else, not here
By this frozen lake —

Or, if here, then I am
Not poet enough
To make the connection.

Are we truly alone
With our physics and myths,
The stars no more

Than glittering dust,
With no one there
To hear our choral odes?

If so, we can start
To ignore the silence
Of the infinite spaces

And concentrate instead
On the infinity
Under our very noses —

The cry at the heart
Of the artichoke,
The gaiety of atoms.

Better to contemplate
The blank page
And leave it blank

Than modify
Its substance by
So much as a pen-stroke.

Woven of wood nymphs,
It speaks volumes
No one will ever write.

I incline my head
To its candour
And weep for our exile.

Dejection Ode

Bone idle, I lie listening to the rain,
Not tragic now nor yet to frenzy bold.
Must I stand out in thunderstorms again
Who have twice come in from the cold?

Antarctica

(for Richard Ryan)

'I am just going outside and may be some time.'
The others nod, pretending not to know.
At the heart of the ridiculous, the sublime.

He leaves them reading and begins to climb,
Goading his ghost into the howling snow;
He is just going outside and may be some time.

The tent recedes beneath its crust of grime
And frostbite is replaced by vertigo:
At the heart of the ridiculous, the sublime.

Need we consider it some sort of crime,
This numb self-sacrifice of the weakest? No,
He is just going outside and may be some time —

In fact, for ever. Solitary enzyme,
Though the night yield no glimmer there will glow,
At the heart of the ridiculous, the sublime.

He takes leave of the earthly pantomime
Quietly, knowing it is time to go.
'I am just going outside and may be some time.'
At the heart of the ridiculous, the sublime.

Kinsale

The kind of rain we knew is a thing of the past —
deep-delving, dark, deliberate you would say,
browsing on spire and bogland; but today
our sky-blue slates are steaming in the sun,
our yachts tinkling and dancing in the bay
like racehorses. We contemplate at last
shining windows, a future forbidden to no one.

Bird Life

The gulls are out at the Old Head
where the *Lusitania* went down
so we make do with rooks instead
among the tiered roofs of the town.
The gulls are out among the fish,
raiding the trawlers at the quay;
crows stride among our spilt rubbish
staring ferociously at the sea.

Dawn at St Patrick's

(*for Terence Brown*)

There is an old
statue in the courtyard
that weeps, like Niobe, its sorrow in stone.
The griefs of the ages she has made her own.
Her eyes are rain-washed but not hard,
her body is covered in mould,
the garden overgrown.

One by one
the first lights come on,
those that haven't been on all night.
Christmas, the harshly festive, has come and gone.
No snow, but the rain pours down
in the first hour before dawn,
before daylight.

Swift's home
for 'fools and mad' has become
the administrative block. Much there
has remained unchanged for many a long year —
stairs, chairs, Georgian windows shafting light and dust,
radiantly white the marble bust
of the satirist;

but the real
hospital is a cheerful
modern extension at the back
hung with restful reproductions of Klee, Dufy and Braque.
Television, Russian fiction, snooker with the staff,
a snifter of Lucozade, a paragraph
of *Newsweek* or the *Daily Mail*

are my daily routine
during the festive season.
They don't lock the razors here
as in Bowditch Hall. We have remained upright —
though, to be frank, the Christmas dinner scene,
with grown men in their festive gear,
was a sobering sight.

I watch the last
planes of the year go past,
silently climbing a cloud-lit sky.
Earthbound, soon I'll be taking a train to Cork
and trying to get back to work
at my sea-lit, fort-view desk
in the turf-smoky dusk.

Meanwhile,
next door, a visiting priest
intones to a faithful dormitory.
I sit on my Protestant bed, a make-believe existentialist,
and stare at the clouds of unknowing. We style,
as best we may, our private destiny;
or so it seems to me

as I chew my thumb
and try to figure out
what brought me to my present state —
an 'educated man', a man of consequence, no bum
but one who has hardly grasped what life is about,
if anything. My children, far away,
don't know where I am today,

in a Dublin asylum
with a paper whistle and a mince pie,
my bits and pieces making a home from home.
I pray to the rain clouds that they never come
where their lost father lies, that their mother thrives
    and that I
may measure up to them
before I die.

Soon a new year
will be here demanding, as before,
modest proposals, resolute resolutions, a new leaf,
new leaves. This is the story of my life,
the story of all lives everywhere,
mad fools wherever we are,
in here or out there.

Light and sane
I shall walk down to the train,
into that world whose sanity we know,
like Swift, to be a fiction and a show.
The clouds part, the rain ceases, the sun
casts now upon everyone
its ancient shadow.

Northern Star

(*for Stewart Parker, obiit 2/11/88*)

Ancestral voices bicker; ghosts
wrestle and dance; indignant hosts
of all persuasions dander down
to throng the lanes of Antrim, Down,
burnished pikes unsheathed from thatch,
sabre and flintlock quick to catch;
still the inspired conspirators
make history in Kelly's Cellars

or at Mac Airt's fort on Cave Hill,
their music above politics still
as starlight shines above a bog
— weaver and printer, ideologue,
children of nature, natural sons
and daughters, trenchant resolutions
echoing in that whin-scented air,
adrift like thistledown elsewhere.

Red dawn, white tide and starry night
dissolve to chaos, heartbreak, 'shite
and lunacy', the hanging man,
nothing whatever gone to plan,
leaving our souls still incomplete
and white noise of sectarian hate
echoing down the continuous past
in the loved entries of Belfast.

Wee corner shops we used to know,
'close-knit communities', the flow
of generational energy, streams
of consciousness, rain-traffic dreams,
the summer bus from glen to glen —
a common enough existence then,
or nearly, till the story broke
and the whole place went up in smoke.

White noise of gulls at rubbish dumps,
killers and victims both at once,
each blow a self-inflicted wound;
and always the holistic sound
of blackbirds on a summer night
in a world transfigured by starlight
— till all fade oblivionwards
'drowning out any further words'.

Noon at St Michael's

Nurses and nuns —
their sails whiter than those
of the yachts in the bay, they come and go
on winged feet, most of them, or in sensible shoes.
July, and I should be climbing among stones
or diving, but for broken bones,
from the rocks below.

I try to read
a new novel set aside;
but a sword-swift pain
in the left shoulderblade, the result
of a tumble in Sheridan Square, makes reading difficult:
writing you can do in your head.
It starts to rain

on the sea,
suddenly dark, the pier,
the gardens and the church spires of Dun Laoghaire.
You would think it was suddenly October
as smoke flaps, the yachts tack violently
and those caught in the downpour
run for cover.

But in a few
minutes the sun shines again,
the leaves and hedges glisten as if with dew
in that fragrant freshness after rain
when the world seems made anew
before confusion, before pain;
and I think of you,

a funny-face
but solemn, with the sharpest mind I know,
a thoughtful creature of unconscious grace

bent to your books in the sun or driving down
to New York for an evening on the town.
Doors open wherever you go
in that furious place;

for you are the light
rising on lost islands, the *spéir-bhean*
the old poets saw gleam in the morning mist.
When you walk down Fifth Avenue in your lavender suit,
your pony eyes opaque, I am the one
beside you, and life is bright
with the finest and best.

And I have seen,
as you have not, such is your modesty,
men turn to watch your tangle of golden hair,
your graceful carriage and unhurried air
as if you belonged to history
or '*her* story', that mystery.
You might have been

a saint or a great
courtesan, anachronistic now
in some ways, in some ways more up-to-date
than the most advanced of those we know.
While you sit on your sun-porch in Connecticut
re-reading Yeats in a feminist light
I am there with you.

Yaddo, or A Month in the Country

(for Rory and Katie)

We are born in an open field and we die in a dark wood.
— Russian proverb

Here among silent lakes and dripping pines
off Route 9P, I write you guys these lines
to ask you what you're up to and what not.
No doubt I'll finish them in my attic flat
in Dublin, if I ever get back there
to the damp gardens of Fitzwilliam Square.
Do you still like your London schools? Do you
still slam the goals in, Rory? Katie-coo,
how goes it with the piano and the flute?
I've a composer in the next-door suite
composing string quartets, an English novelist,
a sculptor from Vermont and a young ceramist
from Kansas; for we come in suns and snows
from *everywhere* to write, paint and compose.
Sport? We've a pool, closed till the end of May,
a tennis court where no one seems to play;
though there's a horse show, among other things,
starting next week in Saratoga Springs
just down the road — a fascinating place
with spas and concerts and a certain grace.
Also a certain measure of renown
since it was here, in an open field north of the town,
that Philip Schuyler clobbered John Burgoyne
in 1777, two hundred and thirteen years ago,
thus helping to precipitate the America we know.
But you're not interested in that kind of stuff;
like me, you'd rather go to the movies for a laugh —
or would you? We talk so infrequently
I hardly know where your real interests lie.
What, for example, are you reading now?
John Buchan? Molly Keane? *Catch-22*?

Nothing too highbrow, time enough for that;
you're better off with a flute or a cricket bat.
You're only (only!) in your middle teens,
too young to be thinking about *seerious* things
like the dream plays and ghost sonatas your
lost father hears and watches everywhere,
especially when he glimpses happy families
a-picnicking among the squirrel trees.
I try to imagine you asleep, at work,
or walking with your mother in Hyde Park
where once we walked each Sunday, hand in hand,
to feed the daffy ducks on the Round Pond,
chucking crumbs to the ones we liked the best,
comical, tufted yellow-eyes, ignoring all the rest.
Remember birthday parties, rockets at Hallowe'en,
bus-rides to Covent Garden to see Eugene?
The day we drove to Brighton? Maybe not.
Summer and winter I would rise and trot
my fingers up your backs like a mad mouse
to wake you chuckling. Now I wake in a silent house
in a dark wood. Once, 'Is it morning time?',
asked Katie waking. Now it is mourning time
in a black heart; but I will not forget
the nooks and corners of our crazy flat,
its dormer windows and its winding stair,
gulls on the roof, its views of *everywhere*!
When Mummy and I split up and I lived in Co. Cork
among the yacht crowd and bohemian folk
I'd wander round the hills above Kinsale
where English forces clobbered Hugh O'Neill
or dander down along the Bandon River
wondering when next we'd be together;
then home to a stable loft where I could hear
mysterious night sounds whispering in my ear —
woodpigeons, foxes, silence, my own brain,
my lamp a lighthouse in the drizzling rain.
After a month of fog a day would dawn

when the rain ceased, cloud cleared and the sun shone;
then magical white wisps of smoke would rise
and I'd think of our own magical London years.
'One always loses with a desperate throw':
what I lost was a wife, a life, and you.
As for love, a treasure when first it's new,
it all too often fades away, for both, like the morning dew;
yet it remains the one sure thing to cling to
as I cling for dear life to the thought of you,
sitting alone here in upstate New York
halfway to Montreal, trying to work,
lit by Tiffany lamps, Sinéad O'Connor on the stereo.
This above all, to thine own selves be true,
remembering seaside games in stormy Ulster parts
and Sunday lunches at the Chelsea Arts
with lemonade for you in paper cups,
snooker and candlelight for the 'grown-ups'.
Your father (yawn!) has seen enough mischance
trying to figure out the dancers from the dance.
Like Mummy, *some* can dance; I never could,
no more than I could ever see the birches for the wood.
We are *all* children; and when either of you
feels scared or miserable, as you must sometimes do,
look to us, but remember we do too.
I hear the big trucks flashing through the night
like Christmas road-houses ablaze with light,
symbols of modern movement and romance;
but the important thing is permanence —
for you, a continuity with the past
enabling you to prosper, and a fast
forward to where the paradoxes grow
like crocuses in our residual snow;
for me, a long devotion to the art
in which you play such an important part,
a long devotion to the difficult Muse
your mother was, despite our difficulties.
Everything thrives in contrariety — no

thesis without antithesis; no black
without its white, like a hot sun on the ice of a Yaddo lake.
Children of light, may your researches be
reflections on this old anomaly;
may you remember, as the years go by
and you grow slowly towards maturity,
that life consists in the receipt of life,
its fun and games, its boredom and its grief;
that no one, sons or daughters, fathers, wives,
escapes the rough stuff that makes up our lives.
Equip yourselves in every way you can
to take it like a woman or a man,
respecting values you've long understood
pertaining to the true, the beautiful and the good.
Sorry to sound so tedious and trite.
I'd hoped to be more fun and try to write
you something entertaining as I often try to do;
but this time round I wanted to be *seerious* and true
to felt experience. My love 2U.
Nothing I say you don't already know.
Football and flute, you'll join us soon enough
in the mad 'grown-up' world of Henry James's 'stupid life'.
Write soon and tell me all about your work.
It's time now for your father to be heading for New York,
a city worse than London, rife with confrontation,
much like the one you see on television.
Maybe I'll read this letter at the 'Y'
and tell you all about it by and by.
I hope I haven't bored you stiff already.
Write to me soon in Dublin.
                    My love, as ever,
                              — Daddy.

New York Time

(for Patricia King)

1

Winter

*Sometimes, from beyond the skyscrapers, the cry of a tugboat
finds you in your insomnia, and you remember this desert of
iron and cement is an island.*
— Albert Camus, *American Journals*

Winter; a short walk from the 10th St. Pier —
and what of the kick-start that should be here?
The fishy ice lies thick on Gansevoort
around the corner, and the snow shines bright
about your country house this morning. Short
the time left to find the serenity
which for a lifetime has eluded me . . .
A rented 'studio apartment' in New York
five blocks from the river, time to think and work,
long-suffering friends and visitors, the bars
where Dylan Thomas spent his final hours,
God rest him; but there's something missing here
in this autistic slammer, some restorative
laid like a magic wand on everything —
on bed, chair, desk and air-conditioner.
I often visualize in the neon slush
that great heart-breaking moment in *The Gold Rush*
where Chaplin, left alone on New Year's Eve,
listens to life's feast from his little shack
and the strains of 'Auld Lang Syne' across the snow.
Oh, show me how to recover my lost nerve!
The radiators knock, whistle and sing.
I toss and turn and listen, when I wake,
to the first bird and the first garbage truck,
seeing the 'lordly' Hudson 'hardly' flow
to New York Harbour and the sea below.

The lights go out along the Jersey shore
and, as Manhattan faces east once more,
dawn's early light on bridge and water tower,
Respighi's temperate nightingale on WQXR
pipes up though stronger stations throng the air —
a radio serendipity to illustrate
the resilience of our lyric appetite,
carnivalesque or studiously apart,
on tap in offices, lofts and desperate 'hoods
to Lorca's 'urinating multitudes'
while I make tea and wait for the ghastly news
at eight; but first the nightingale. Sing, Muse.

2

Out There

Left completely to his own devices, the bachelor's idea of interior decoration is a pyramid of empty beer cans on a window-ledge.
— P. J. O'Rourke, *The Bachelor Home Companion*

Here I was, sitting quietly in my studio
and grading papers with the radio low
as Pascal says we should, when out of the blue
last night, under the fire-escape, some psycho
sends up a stream of picturesque abuse
directed, evidently, at my 4th-floor window,
his reasoning trenchant, complex and abstruse —
one of those paranoids who seem to know
the system's out to get them even so;
for paranoia, of course, is no excuse.
A nervous terrier, left home alone
and maddened, maybe, by the relentless tone,
went crazy, hollering in the flat below;
then it was time for the lunatic upstairs
to shift his desk and re-align his chairs;
a *West Side Story* love scene on the sidewalk,
whoop of police sirens, car alarms
unanimous as in a California quake
while most lay dreaming in each others' arms.
Around five a hand, with Gershwin nonchalance,
shook up the empties in the recycling bin
at the corner, shivering for a drop of gin,
its movements brisk, fastidious and, all at once,
triumphant . . . Dawn; the kick-start as some heroine
draws on her gloves for the Yamaha dream trip
to Provincetown, Key West or Sunset Strip.
Tired vents exhale; cloudy windows condense;
vague vapours pearl fire hydrant and chain-link fence;
and the homeless gaze with satire or indifference
from cardboard boxes on a construction site
as she sets out on her epic expedition.

163

To each his haste; to each his dreamt occasion.
Nor snow, nor rain, nor sleet, nor gloom of night
stays these swift couriers from their appointed flight.

3

Global Village

This morning, from beyond abandoned piers
where the great liners docked in former years,
a foghorn echoes in deserted sheds
known to Hart Crane, and in our vigilant beds.
No liners now, nothing but ice and grime,
a late flame flickering on Brodsky St. News time
in the global village — Ethiopian drought,
famine, whole nations, races, evicted even yet,
rape victim and blind beggar at the gate —
the images forming which will be screened tonight
on CNN and *The McNeil-Lehrer News Hour*,
the sense of being right there on the spot —
a sense I get right here that Gansevoort
has 'no existence, natural or real, apart
from its being perceived by the understanding'. Not
that I seriously doubt the reality of the Hudson Bar
and Diner; but the skills of Venturi, Thompson, Rowse
that can make post-modern a 19th-century warehouse
and those of Hollywood *film noir* have combined
to create virtual realities in the mind
so the real thing tells us what we already know
behind the signs. Obviously I don't mean
to pen yet one more craven European
paean to the States, nor would you expect me to,
not being a yuppie in a pinstripe suit
but an Irish bohemian even as you are too
though far from the original 'Ballroom of Romance',
far too from your posh convent school in France.
Out here in the clear existential light
I miss the half-tones we're accustomed to:
an amateur immigrant, sure I like the corny
humanism and car-stickers — 'I♡NY' —
and yet remain sardonic and un-*chic*,
an undesirable resident alien on this shore,
a face in the crowd in this offshore boutique

inscribed with the ubiquitous comic-strip blob-speak
— LOVE ONE ANOTHER, RESIST INSIPID RHYME —
exposed in thunderstorms, as once before,
and hoping to draw some voltage one more time.

4

Waterfront

We shall go down like palaeolithic man
Before some new Ice Age or Genghiz Khan.
                    — Louis MacNeice, 'An Eclogue for Christmas'

Chaste convalescents from an exigent world,
we come to rivers when we are young or old;
stir-crazy, driven by cabin fever, I choose
the 10th St. Pier and toddle into the cold.
Where once the waters spun to your fierce screws
— *Nieuw Amsterdam, Caronia, Île de France* —
ice inches seaward in a formal dance
where now, adrift with trash and refuse barges,
the photo-realist estuary 'discharges
its footage' into the blind Atlantic snow.
Smoky and crepitant, glacier-spiky, rough
in its white logic, it is a lithograph
from *The Ancient Mariner*, from *Scott's Last Voyage*
or *The Narrative of Arthur Gordon Poe*;
and old Heraclitus might have walked here too.
This morning, though, the throes of a warm snap
so ice cracks far off like a thunderclap
somewhere along Bohemia's desert coast
and puffs drift in the white riparian light,
gunsmoke against storm clouds in the west
that rain infection and industrial waste,
though now we emerge from the industrial night;
and I recall my ten-year-old delight
at the launch of a P&O liner in Belfast,
all howling 'O God, Our Help in Ages Past',
tugs hooting, block and tackle thundering into the tide.
I can hear no Jersey blackbird serenade
this rapt scribe gazing from the Big Apple side;
yet, having come so far from home,
I try to imagine our millennium
where, in the thaw-water of an oil drum,

the hot genes of the future seethe. The sun
shines on the dump, not on the *côte d'azur*
and not on the cloistered murals, to be sure.
— SUBVERT THE DOMINANT PARADIGM. GABRIEL 141.

5

'To Mrs Moore at Innishannon'

*The sculptor reacted with horror to the prospect of immigrants
landing near his masterpiece; he called it 'a monstrous plan'. So
much for Emma Lazarus ...*
                    — Mary Gordon, *Good Boys and Dead Girls*

No. 1, 5th Avenue, New York City, Sept. 14th, 1895
— and Mother, dear, I'm glad to be alive
after a whole week on the crowded *Oceanic* —
tho' I got here all right without being sick.
We boarded in the rain, St Colman's spire
shrinking ashore, a few lamps glimm'ring there
(*'Will the last to leave please put out the lights?'*),
and slept behind the engine for six nights.
A big gull sat at the masthead all the way
from Roche's Point to Montock, till one day
it stagger'd up and vanish'd with the breeze
in the mass'd rigging by the Hudson quays ...
Downtown, dear God, is like a glimpse of Hell
in a 'hot wave': drunken men, the roaring 'El',
the noise and squalour indescribable.
(Manners are rough and speech indelicate;
more teeming shore than you cd. shake a stick at.)
However, the Kellys' guest-house; church and tram;
now, thanks to Mrs O'Brien, here I am
at last, install'd amid the kitchenware
in a fine house a short step from Washington Square.
Protestants, mind you, and a bit serious,
much like the Bandon sort, not crack like us,
the older children too big for their britches
tho' Sam, the 4-yr.-old, has me in stitches:
in any case, the whole country's under age.
I get each Sunday off and use the privilege
to explore Broadway, the new Brooklyn Bridge
or the statue of Liberty, copper torch on top
which, wd. you believe it, actually lights up,

and look at the Jersey shoreline, blue and gold:
it's all fire and sunlight here in the New World.
Eagles and bugles! Curious their simple faith
that stars and stripes are all of life and death —
as if Earth's centre lay in Central Park
when we both know it runs thro' Co. Cork.
Sometimes at night, in my imagination,
I hear you calling me across the ocean;
but the money's good, tho' I've had to buy new clothes
for the equatorial climate. I enclose
ten dollars, more to come (here, for God's sake,
they fling the stuff around like snuff at a wake).
'Bye now; and Mother, dear, you may be sure
I remain
      yr. loving daughter,
                  — Bridget Moore.

6

The Bronx Seabirds

INSIDER TRADING REPORTS ARE LINKED TO PRICE OF BONDS
NO SOLUTION AT HAND WHILE NUCLEAR WASTE PILES UP
NEW YORK TOUGHING IT OUT TO GET THROUGH THE COLD
QUESTION REALITY DEATH IS BACK NIGHT OWL GABRIEL 141
AT&T BOEING CHRYSLER DUPONT DIGITAL DOW JONES
EXXON GENERAL MOTORS IBM NYNEX SEARS
PARANOIA McCANN ERICKSON AMERICA AFTER DARK
ESCAPED BRONX SEABIRDS SPOTTED IN CENTRAL PARK . . .
. . . On ledge and rail they sit, Inca tern and Andean gull, who
fled their storm-wrecked cage in the Bronx Zoo
and now flap in exhilaration and growing fear
above Yonkers, New Rochelle, Great Neck, Astoria,
Long Beach, Red Hook, Bay Ridge, the whole 'tri-state area',
a transmigration of souls, crazy-eyed as they peer
through mutant cloud cover and air thick with snow-dust,
toxic aerosol dazzle and invasive car exhaust,
or perch forlorn on gargoyle and asbestos roof,
fine-featured, ruffled, attentive, almost too high to hear
the plaintive, desolate cab horns on Madison and Fifth:
like Daisy's Cunard nightingale, they belong in another life.
They are intrigued, baffled and finally bored stiff
by the wised-up millions lunching far below
but vulnerable too as, askance, they stare
at the alien corn of Radio City, Broadway and Times Square
and up again at the clouds: where on earth can they go?
They 'won't touch garbage'; so where and what will they eat?
If you see one of these nervous birds on ledge or sill
(dark blue, light grey, white head and tail, red bill),
contact the Manhattan Avian Rehab Centre
— (212) 689-3039 — and ask for Clare or Jill;
though, to be frank, their chances are less than fair
nor, to be honest, is our confidence great
that these rare species will be fit to compete
in the fight for survival on the city street
with urban gulls, crows, and other toughs of the air.

7

The Travel Section

(after Laforgue)

I'm reading about life on the prairie and frontier
when a voice cries: 'Hey, you could live here!'
Outcast from the old world, a desperado
without God or government, where could I not go?
Out there I'll scalp my European brain,
run wild like a young colt on the open plain —
a sort of post-literate, Huck Finn child of nature
or existential citizen of the future,
an idealistic rustic, rancher, architect,
hunter, fisherman, gambler, prickly autodidact;
and live, buckskin-clad, on whiskey and pot-roast
between Colorado and the Pacific Coast,
sleeping out under pre-Columbian skies
more generous than our bourgeois certainties!
And? A mystique of campsites, the 'Lynch' law,
rough diamonds to clutch in my grubby paw,
a gold rush over the desert at first light,
a poker school around the fire at night . . .
When I grow old, a farm in the sunrise,
a dairy cow, grandchildren at my knees
and, slung from the twin cow horns over the gate,
a split-pine signboard advertising 'Body Art'.
And if fond memories of the Place Vendôme
or the high hopes of my contemporaries
should tempt me into thoughts of going home
I'd start a new cult of the Golden Age
with its own code based on holistic books,
blithe and post-modern, for the post-pastoral folks.

8

Ovid on West 4th

*Women are necessarily capable of almost anything in their struggle
for survival and can scarcely be convicted of such man-made crimes
as 'cruelty'.*
    — F. Scott Fitzgerald, *Tender is the Night*

When his wronged wife Procne sat him down to eat
King Tereus little knew what was on his plate.
(Afternoon now, some silence in the street
till released children dash to bus and swing.)
Pretending this dinner was a traditional thing,
an Athenian feast fit only for a king,
she excused the servants. Throned in his royal seat,
poor Tereus sipped his wine in solitary state
and, forking his own son hot from a covered dish,
called out: 'Hey, send young Itys here to me!'
Procne could barely conceal her wicked glee
and answered, keen to tell him the bad news,
pointing at Tereus' stomach, 'There he is!'
'What do you mean?' says Tereus, looking foolish,
'I don't see him.' Then, as he called once more,
fair Philomela appeared, dripping with blood, and flung
Itys' severed head, itself streaming with gore,
right in Tereus' face, as he picked at his own young.
Oh, how she longed then for the use of her tongue!
Nothing would have given her greater pleasure
than to whisper a few harsh words to her ravisher;
as for the king, he nearly had a seizure
to think that he should eat his . . . own son Itys.
Howling, he swept aside the candlesticks
and called the furies from the depths of Styx —
no, howling he overturned the dinner table
and called the furies from the hobs of hell.
Unhinged to think this flesh of his own flesh
consumed by the viscera where the genes first grew
and he his own son's charnel house, he drew

his sword to open his own digestive tract
and pluck the chewed-up gobbets from the mush
but turned instead on the two sisters, who fled
as if on wings; and they *were* winged, in fact,
both of them changed in a twinkling into birds
whirring and twittering inches above his head,
swallow and nightingale hovering in mid-air.
One flew to the rooftop, one flew to the woods,
and even today the nightingale can be heard
descanting in convent garden and Georgian square.
Tereus, with hair on end and furious sword-bill,
turned into a hoopoe and is furious still . . .
. . . Never mind the hidden agenda, the sub-text;
it's not really about male arrogance, 'rough sex'
or vengeful sisterhood, but about art
and the encoded mysteries of the human heart.

9

London Time

'Nature, not having included me in her plan,
has treated me like an uninvited guest'
— Turgenev, *Diary of a Superfluous Man.*
You call home while I take my daily rest.
It's 9.00 p.m. London time when your mother
picks up the phone 3,000 miles away
in Shepherd's Bush. Dinner is nearly over
perhaps, and the BBC on the news-box
(Soviet disintegration, 'Anglo-Irish' talks)
as it used to be, while on the sofa lie
new fiction, Jacobean drama, philosophy,
the *Observer* magazine and the *Daily Mail.*
— I'm guessing . . . Tell me, son, do you recall,
ten years ago now, when our 'little platoon'
would march round Barrie's pond each afternoon?
Here early for the World Cup and having a ball,
you talk to your sister now in that lost domain
describing how, holed up in a brownstone
on St Luke's Place, and painting the house in lieu
of rent, you're off to a party below Canal
with friends in the film scene and the rock milieu.
Today, across 3,000 miles of water
and five time zones, my own prayer for my daughter
would be, not innocence and ceremony
exactly, but a more complicated grace,
the sort of thing you play when you're alone,
Katie, something slow and meditative,
some rich myth of reconciliation
as if a statue moved and began to live —
for I like to think all this is a winter's tale.
A precocious feminist, already at the age of five
contemptuous of your raggedy dolls, derisive
but *seerious* of course, you were a scream,
therefore a born artist; but even the *being* is an art
we learn for ourselves, in solitude, on our very own,

listening to the innermost silence of the heart,
prolonging the inconsequence of a gaze
and dreaming at all times our uninterruptible dream
of redemptive form. I saw a film recently,
Glenn Gould playing Bach to the Canadian wilderness,
the great chords crashing out into empty space,
the music of the planet, the glorious racket
with which we explain ourselves in perpetuity
to our hi-tech geological posterity
at the frozen outer reaches of the galaxy.
It's ridiculous but *just do it*, as they say here;
make noise without embarrassment or fear. Take it
from the top, Katie; yours is the sound we want to hear!

10

St Mark's Place

Auden, slop-slippered bear of St Mark's Place,
I seem to glimpse your cheesy limestone face
as you stand at your dirty window, gin in paw,
on a hot evening during the great Cold War
where the young Trotsky published *Novy Mir*.
Joseph the druggist, Abe in the liquor store,
Maurice the mailman and Marianne Moore
are the happier for your grumpy love; for, funny
in Hobbit sweatshirt and dubious Levi's, you
were a victim of nothing but irony, Gramsci's new
'disease of the interregnum'; and to castration-
and-death phone threats replied without hesitation:
'I think you've the wrong number.' A disgrace
to the neighbourhood, insistent on your privacy,
what would you make now of the cosmic *pax
Americana*, our world of internet and fax,
an ever more complex military-industrial complex,
situational ethics, exonerative 12-step programs,
health fascism, critical theory and 'smart' bombs?
While we hole up in our bath-houses and catacombs,
votaries of Eros if not always of Aphrodite,
I see you ride at rush hour with your rich pity
and self-contempt an uptown train packed to the doors
with 'aristocratic Negro faces', not like ours,
or reciting 'The Unknown Citizen' at the 'Y'.
When will she — Gaia, Clio — send downpours
to silence the 'gnostic chirrup' of her calumniators?
When will we hear once more the pure voice of elation
raised in the nightwood of known symbol and allusion?
So far from mothers, in the unmarried city,
you contemplate a new ode to Euphrosyne,
goddess of banquets; and in the darkest hours
of holocaust and apocalypse, cheap music and singles bars,
you remind us of what the examined life involves —
for what you teach is the courage to be ourselves,

however ridiculous; and if you were often silly
or too 'prone to hold forth', you prescribe a cure
for our civilization and its discontents
based upon *agapè*, baroque opera, common sense
and the abstract energy that brought us here,
sustaining us now as we face a more boring future.

11

Chinatown

The wind of the common people whirls from lanes and alleys,
poking the rubbish, stirring up the dust . . .
                                    — Hsiang Ch'u, 3rd c.

. . . and whips the pagodas of Confucius Square.
GABRIEL 141. EAT THE RICH. FIND THE CURE.
A rackety sunset under a storm-lit sky
where we sit, uncool dad and laconic son,
amid the festive clatter of Son Low Kee,
dining on midnight mussels and sesame prawn
torn from the hairy darkness of the sea.
A crackle of firecrackers all over the ward
for the Chinese New Year, Gambino and Genovese
having moved on. 'Where the broom fails to reach,'
said Mao, 'the dust won't clear of its own accord';
but we like it here in this ethnocentric refuge
under the fairy lights of Brooklyn Bridge
where the quiet or chattering families sit at board.
We're one of the quiet tables as we review
your temporary job, tonight's occasion.
You're listening to Guns 'n' Roses, Simple Minds, U2
and reading *Moby Dick*, according to you;
but I recognize your strategies of evasion
for I too was young and morose, in youth
a frightful little shit to tell the truth,
a rancorous paragon of bile and sloth
in the days of nihilism and alienation;
in any event, those ancient days are gone
like the T'ang Dynasty and the shoes of 1941.
We're all lost boys, or so we like to imagine —
and being young, I remember it well, is tough:
will the last bus be gone, her light be on or off?
I wouldn't do it again for all the tea in Taiwan;
but, now you've reached the age of rock and soccer
and I the age of 'serious medicine',

let me, Polonius of the twilight zone,
offer you some belated, functional succour.
I need hardly speak to you in praise of women
since you grew up amongst them. (So did I
but there's a tale will keep indefinitely.)
Be thou familiar but by no means vulgar; shun
the fatuous rectitude of received opinion,
newspeak and euphemism. Don't 'stick up for your rights'
or worry about your self-esteem; contrive
your own life and live it by your own lights
where such considerations don't apply.
Costly thy habit as thy purse can buy.
Be sceptical but wholehearted; don't be shy;
trust your own instincts, even the most fugitive;
and welcome to *la condition humaine*.
Cheer up, son; oh, and above all disbelieve
the cynic who tries to tell you how to behave
for, as Confucius said, fine words are seldom humane.

12

Alien Nation

*These chronic homeless are mostly single adults who have given
up seeking help because they feel the 'system' has given up on them
and is largely unresponsive to their needs. Many are substance
abusers . . . Getting high or drunk may be the only way they know
of alleviating their pain and disappointment.*
— *What You Can Do to Help the Homeless*
(Simon & Schuster, 1991)

RX GOTHAM DRUG GAY CRUISES SONY LIQUORS MARLBORO
ADULT VIDEO XXX BELSHAZZAR DEATH IS BACK
IGLESIA ADVENTISTA DEL 7MO. DIA . . .
. . . We come upon them in the restless dark
in the moon-shadow of the World Trade Centre
with Liberty's torch glimmering over the water,
glued to a re-run of *The Exterminator*
on a portable TV in a corner of Battery Park
(some have park views, others sleep in the park),
and think how sensible the alternative polity
beneath the ostensible, pharaonic city
glimpsed through rain or dust from an expressway —
the old clothes, packing cases and auto trunks
seen everywhere from here to the South Bronx,
its population growing by the week, by the day,
oblivious to our chaos theories and data banks,
from the Port Authority Bus Terminal to JFK
and farther afield, in freight-yard and loading bay,
gull-screaming landfill, stripped trailer and boxcar,
the gap increasing between the penthouse tower
and the desert of cinderblock and razor wire
behind the Ritz-Carlton or Holiday Inn.
We are all survivors in this rough terrain;
I know you and you me, you wretched buggers,
and I've no problem calling you my brothers
for I too have been homeless and in detox
with BAAAD niggaz 'n' crack hoes on the rocks.

Blown here like particles from an exploding sun,
we are all far from home, be our home still
a Chicago slum, a house under the Cave Hill
or a trailer parked in a field above Cushendun.
Clutching our bits and pieces, arrogant in dereliction,
we are all out there, filling the parks and streets
with our harsh demand: 'Sleep faster, we need the sheets!'
Now off to your high loft in the disco night,
young faces glittering under trippy light,
smoke red and yellow where the doctor spins
high-octane decks among the boogie bins.
An ocean breeze, flower-scented, soft and warm,
blows downtown where we part in the night air;
a Haitian driver, mordant as Baudelaire,
whisks me up Hudson St. in a thunderstorm.

13

Sappho in 'Judith's Room'

What is important now is to recover our senses; in place of a hermeneutics we need an erotics of art.
— Susan Sontag, *Against Interpretation* (1964)

The reed-voiced nightingale has been my guide,
soft-spoken announcer of spring, whose song I set
against a cult of contention I decried —
except, of course, for 'the fight to be affectionate'.
A corps of men, a list of ships? Give me instead
my non-violent girls — Cydro, Gongula — and particularly
our glamorous Anactoria somewhere over the sea
whose eyes' mischievous sparkle remains to me
a finer sight than Homeric bronze; for now,
like the moon rising at sunset, casting its glow
on the waves, on evening meadows of brine and dew,
she climbs the night sky, and perhaps her heart too
is heavy with recollection, perhaps out there she hears
the wind among the reeds, and calls, so the soft-petal'd ears
of darkness hear her, and the dividing sea.
Aphrodite, weaver of intrigue, revisit my heart
as so often before in your dove-drawn chariot.
Nothing was alien to me, nothing inhuman:
what did I teach but the love of women?
Soon, when the moon and Pleiades have gone,
in the vast silence of the night I shall lie alone
or sit, tenth Muse, in this American bookstore
relishing the historical ironies in store
and the 'homeless flow of life' beyond the door.
The authors are all women, and I myself
am represented on the poetry shelf
(miraculously, I hold here in my hands
fragments exhumed from the Egyptian sands);
for if harsh nature made me short and dark
she picked me out to do immortal work.

Before the *cafeneion* I'd sit when young
in sea-girt Mytilene of the dirty dances
making eye contact with new acquaintances
and relishing our sweet Aeolian tongue;
and, now that I exceed in fame our fine
Alcaeus, the laureate of politics and wine
whose high style was more 'serious' than mine,
the bad girls of my cult, an ardent choir
whose shafts shivered their music in my lyre,
votaries of Aphrodite, a thoughtful crowd,
still gather here to hear me read aloud;
and if I cling still to an old favouritism
or fall for a younger man from time to time
I'm happiest here in a place like Judith's Room
with Djuna, Janis, Gloria, Brooke and Kim.
Girls all, be with me now and keep me warm —
didn't I *say* we'd live again in another form?

14

Beauty and the Beast

'I don't know any stories; none of the lost boys know any stories.'
'How perfectly awful,' said Wendy.
                                        — J. M. Barrie, *Peter Pan*

I go night-shopping like Frank O'Hara I go bopping
up Bleecker for juice, croissants, Perrier, ice-cream
and Gitane *filtre*, pick up the laundry, get back
to five (5!) messages on the answering machine
from Mary K. and Eliza, Louis, Barry and Jack,
and on TV sixty channels of mind-polluting dreck.
Thank God for the VCR. Now at last I can screen
the old movies I haven't seen since I was young —
A Night to Remember, Rear Window, High Noon,
The Man Who Never Was, A King in New York . . .
Tonight, for example, tickled to bits, I stick on
the 'original, uncut' version of *King Kong*:
childish, perhaps, but a cultural critic's dream.
I rewind, fast-forward, and replay the scene
where Kong instals Fay Wray screaming on the high rock
where he lives, and she's attacked by a griffin, roc,
velociraptor, hoopoe, some such creation,
a thousand feet above the Indian Ocean,
wherever, and you can see the little freighter
waiting far out there on the sparkling water.
Sensitive Kong doesn't interfere with her sexually
though he does *paw* and sniff his fingers, actually,
eyes bright with curiosity; then the entire cast
come tough-talking through the primeval rain forest,
chivalrous Robert Armstrong sets her free
and they run off together down to the shore,
indignant Kong chasing them with a roar
because the poor sap really loves her, do you see.
I sit here like an old child with a new toy
or a creature from outer space, Saturn perhaps,
admiring the ingenuity of the planet of the apes

when (look!) the huge gorilla, the size of a fly
('Eighth Wonder of the World', says the publicity),
climbs up, like Batman, the side of the Empire State,
a black speck outlined against the morning sky.
It's all inconsistent, of course, and disproportionate,
he's too small there and too big on the street, *I know*,
but it makes no difference, it's a magnificent show.

   The little bi-planes come gunning for him now
and Kong, by Jove, knocks one of them out of the sky
with a hairy hand. They wear him out, of course,
and he falls to extinction among the crowds below.
And Fay??? She screams but she's safe; it might've been worse.
I breathe again and zap, lord of the universe,
the credits. Semiotician, couch potato,
I've had them all here in my room on video —
Leigh, Grahame, Taylor, Kelly and Monroe.
Fay, born in Alberta, you were also in *Dirigible*
and 'existed most forcefully when faced with terror'
says *Video Guide* — like most of us, probably. Well,
Kong and I dedicate this one to you, old girl,
wherever you are; pushing ninety and hanging in there,
we want you to know we love you and think of you still.

                                        (*for Fay Wray*)

15

A Starlit Corner

Now that we all get laid and everyone swings,
who needs the formal continence of *l'amour
courtois* and the hang-ups of a provincial clique
before innocence died at Béziers and Montségur?
Still, in the brisk heart a faint voice will speak,
in a starlit corner of the soul there sings
to an enclosed loved one the intense troubadour
in his quaint language, and his rondeau rings
resiliently on the vineyards, streams and rock-
strewn hillsides of 12th-century Languedoc;
still in her forest tower under the wild rain
of Poitiers, Limoges, Dordogne or Aquitaine
there sleeps the remote, enfamilied chatelaine
while Riquier, Bornheil, Vidal and Uc St-Cir,
the accomplished amateur and the shivering boy
render, beneath her window, a 'chaste' homage.
The sun goes down beyond the known world's edge
and a crescent moon climbs an incurious sky;
as to the kind of love we mean, they say,
one must be patient, such is its quality.

   Perhaps all this was a deplorable thing,
a vicious fiction or a coercive myth —
*but when the earth renews itself in spring
and whitethorn flowers to hear the blackbird sing
I too sing, although she whom I admire
finds little to her taste in what I write.
I praise not only her clear skin and fine eyes
but also her frank speech and distinguished air;
so dumbstruck am I on her visiting days
I can find no words to speak of my desire
yet, when she leaves me, my composure flees.
No one I know can hold a candle to her
and when the world dims, as it does tonight,
I see the house she goes to blaze with light.*

16

Key West

Somewhere along Route 1 — Plantation, Tavernier —
cloud-splitting Angie broke over the Keys last year
in June, the earliest ever, bringing torrential rains,
though it wasn't one of those really *terrible* hurricanes
you hear about, that wreck towns and wreak atrocities
on isolated farms, snug harbours, close communities,
but a swift cloud-stream of premonitory showers
that waltzed off in the direction of New Orleans
irrigating pine and cedar, lemon groves and sandbars
while the Bahamas heaved in still-turbulent seas.
The outskirts of Key West, when we got there,
you driving, a white bandana in your hair
and Satchmo growling from the car radio,
were still where they were supposed to be, and calm
between downpours red poinciana, jasmine, palm
and the white frame houses built a century ago
by tough skippers against cyclone and tornado.
The town gasped in a tropical heatwave
and I recalled old Mr Temple's narrative
in *Key Largo*, the great nameless storm of 1935
that killed 800 people, it did too, and blew
the East Coast Railroad into the ocean — true,
the bridges are still standing, but that was the last train.
Suave mari magno turbantibus aequora ventis
e terra magnum alterius spectare laborem:
it's cool, when gale-force winds trouble the waters,
to watch from shore the tribulations of others.

　　Uh-oh, before dawn it came round again,
fat drops hitting on storm lanterns, demented budgies
screeching beyond the pool and the churning trees;
and I pictured the vast turmoil undersea,
a mute universe of sponge and anemone,
of conch and snapper, octopus and algae,
odd fish of every stripe in their coral conservatories,

while counting the chimes of St Mary's, Star of the Sea.
Later, exhausted hens on the telephone lines,
dishevelled dogs in the flooded Bahamian lanes:
chaos, *triste tropique* — till, mauve and rose,
flecked with pistachio cloud, a new kind of day arose
and I saw why once to these shores came other cold
solitaries down from the north in search of love and poetry
to sing in the crashing, galaxy-lit sea porches.
It was one of those far-out, raw mornings, the beaches
strewn with wrack, and a derelict dawn moon,
mountains and craters in visible cameo, yearned
close to the earth as if murmuring to return,
a wreckers' morning, with everyone a bit lost
as if landed from Senegal or the Ivory Coast.

Why so soon in the season? Radio and TV
spoke of 'El Niño', the fabulous, hot tide-thrust
born in December off Peru like the infant Christ
sea-changing *all* with its rough magic; and advised
of hurricanes to come, so that one feared not only
for Cuban cabin and gimcrack condominium
but for the 'sleek and effortless vacation home'
featured in the current issue of *Key Design*,
the 'storm-resistant' dream house with its 'vinyl membrane',
a bait fridge and 'teak tarpon-fighting chair';
for roads and bridges, lighthouses, any structure
presumed permanent; towns and cities everywhere
vulnerable to a trickle of sand, to a breath of fresh air;
and thought of the fragility of all architecture,
the provisional nature even of aerospace.
I keep on my desk here a coarse handful of Florida sea gorse
and remember, this wintry night, that summery place —
how we strolled out there on the still-quaking docks
shaken but exhilarated, turned to retrace
our steps up Caroline St., and sat in Pepe's
drinking rum and Coke with retired hippies
who long ago gave up on the land and settled among the rocks.

17

St Bridget's Day

A roof over my head, protected from the rain,
I'm reading, pilgrim father, your letters to your son
and wondering if, unlike you, I should head for home.
Escaping the turbulence of this modern Rome
in a flurry of skyline views and exploding foam,
I can see that 747 in flight over Nova Scotia,
Lahinch and Limerick, snoring back to the future;
I can see the old stormy island from the air,
its meteorological gaiety and despair,
some evidence of light industry and agriculture,
familiar contours, turfsmoke on field and town;
I can even hear the cabin crew's soft *'fáilte'*
and the strains of 'My Lagan Love' as we touch down.
A recovering Ulster Protestant from Co. Down,
I shall walk the Dublin lanes as the days grow shorter,
I who once had poems in *The New Yorker*,
and spend old age, if any, in an old mac
with the young audibly sneering behind my back,
deafened by seagulls and the playground cries
of children — ourselves, once — by perilous seas.
Now, listening to the *rus-in-urbe*, spring-in-winter noise
of late-night diners while the temperatures rise
and the terrible wind-chill factor abates, I realize
the daffodils must be out in ditch and glen
and windows soon flung wide to the spring rain;
and marvel how, a figure out of the past,
an old man in a hurry, you stuck it here to the last,
negotiating the icefields of 8th Avenue
to die on West 29th of the 'Asian' flu.

But first you met by chance at the riverside
a young woman with a sick child she tried to hide
(not out of shame, you felt, but anguished pride),
soft-spoken, 'from Donnybrook', amid the alien corn.
'It pained me that her bright image should fade.'

Thus your epiphany, and you wrote to explain:
'The nightingale sings with its breast against a thorn,
it's out of pain that personality is born.'
Things you understood: children, the human face,
'something finer than honesty', the kindness
of women and the priority of the real.
Things that puzzled you: economy, fear,
the argument from design, the need to feel secure,
the belief in another world besides this one here.
Despite your rationalism, did it ever appear
that the universe might be *really* 'magical', sir,
and you yourself a showing-forth of that soul?
'Art is dreamland.' When you rejoined the whole
what glimpse was given to you in the black hole?
Now, to 'Yeats, Artist and Writer', may we add
that you were at home here and in human nature
but also, in your own words, lived and died
like all of us, then as now, 'an exile and a stranger'?

18

Rain

Once upon a time it was let me out and let me go —
the night flight over deserts, amid cloud,
a dream of discipline and fit solitude.
Now, drifters, loners, harsh and disconsolate,
'inane and unappeased', we come knocking late;
and now it's take me back and take me in.
So take us in where we set out long ago,
the enchanted garden in the lost domain,
the vigilant lamplight glimpsed through teeming rain,
the house, the stove in the kitchen, the warm bed,
the hearth, *vrai lieu*, ranged crockery overhead,
'felicitous space' lost to the tribes. I lodge
one window slightly open to let in the night air
— ten below, these nights, on average —
heating the street, the clouds, the stratosphere,
and peer down through the fire escape. It's broad
day all night on the 24-hr. film-set,
kliegs bright on stadium and construction site;
but a civilization based on superfluous light
concedes no decent dark, so we create
with blinds and blankets our own private night
to keep the glare out. Searchlights and dead stars
pick out the Trump Tower and the United Nations,
the halls of finance, the subway walls of the brain,
the good, the bad, the ugly and the insane,
the docks and Governor's Island; and the bars
where the lost and the disappointed feel no pain
are empty except for the all-night populations,
no homes to go to but their eternal one.
This is the hour of the chained door and the locked gate,
harsh blues of the rowdy and the unfortunate,
and the fetishes are wakeful in their places —
lamp, chair, desk, oil-heater and bookcases
brisk with a bristling, mute facticity
connecting them to the greater community

of wood and minerals throughout the city.
When the present occupant is no longer here
and durables prove transient, as they do,
all will survive somehow; the pictures too,
prints, posters, reproductions, such as they are:
the obvious sea-born, shell-borne Aphrodite,
Dunluce, 'The Doors of Dublin', Whitman in a suit,
Monet skiffs on the Seine, a window by Bonnard,
Leech's convent garden, a Hopper light,
Hokusai's wave, Lichtenstein's *ingénue*
shedding a tear ('B . . . but, Brad . . .') beside the door
and (look!) my favourite, over there on the right,
picked up at a yard-sale in Connecticut,
Kroyer's *Women on the Beach*, a hazy shore,
their footprints in the sand to the waterline,
the human presence since we live here too —
all primal images in their different ways
watching for springtime and the lengthening days.

    Jequirity, monkshood, nightshade, celandine.
The friends and contemporaries begin to go
— Nina Gilliam, Eugene Lambe, and others too.
'A dry soul is best'; and at night to lie
empty of mind, the heart at peace; *and thou,*
dark mother, cave of wonders, open now
to our languor the interior of the rose
that closes round volition, and disclose
your secret, be it Byzantium or the sphere
all centre, no circumference . . . I pretend
you're here beside me; guardian angel, best friend,
practitioner of tough love and conservation,
I'd say make all safe and harmonious in the end
did I not know the voyage is never done
for, even as we speak, somewhere a plane
gains altitude in the moon's exilic glare
or a car slips into gear in a silent lane . . .
I think of the homeless, no rm. at the inn;

far off, the gaseous planets where they spin,
the starlit towers of Nineveh and Babylon,
the secret voice of nightingale and dolphin,
fish crowding the Verrazano Bridge; and see,
even in the icy heart of February,
crocus and primrose. When does the thaw begin?
We have been too long in the cold. — Take us in; take us in!

Decadence

1

Night Thoughts

Night thoughts are best, the ones that visit us
where we lie smoking between three and four
before the first bird and the first tour bus.
Once you would wake up shaking at this hour
but now, this morning, you are a child once more
wide-eyed in an attic room behind the shore
at some generic, gull-pierced seaside town
in wartime Co. Antrim or Co. Down —
navies aglow off Bangor and Whitehead,
dark sea, Glenn Miller's 'Moonlight Serenade',
huge transport planes thundering overhead.
Each white shoe you can remember, each stair rod,
each streaming window on the Antrim Road,
a seaside golf links on a summer night,
'pale sand dunes stretching away in the moonlight'.
A horse-drawn cab out of the past goes past
toward Leeson St. Night thoughts are best and worst.
My attic window under the shining slates
where maids slept in the days of Wilde and Yeats
sees crane light where the 'construction industry'
throws up new office blocks against the sky.
The place a Georgian theme park for the tourist,
not much remains; though still the first of dawn
whitens a locked park, lilac and hawthorn
dripping in wintry peace, a secret garden
absorbed since the end of summer in its own
existence, gulls driven inland by sea mist.
Soon crocus, daffodil, air brake and diesel-chug,
those rain-washed April mornings when the fog
lifts and immediate 'coaches' throng the square.
Even in the bath I hear them shouting out there —
aliens, space invaders clicking at the front door,
goofy in baseball caps and nylon leisurewear.

Sententious solitude, ancient memory, night
and silence, nobody here; but even as I night-write
blind in a bedside notebook, 'impersonal moonlight
audible on steps, railings, sash window and fanlight',
my biro breaks the silence and something stirs.
Never mind the new world order and the bus tours,
you can still switch on the fire, kick off your shoes
and read the Symbolists as the season dies:
Now for the coughing in school dormitories,
the hot drink far from home. November brings
statistics, papers, cocoa, medicine, dreams,
windows flung wide on briny balconies
above an ocean of roofs and lighthouse beams;
like a storm lantern the lonely planet swings.

2

Axel's Castle

A mature artist takes the material closest to hand.
— George Moore

Rain all day, now clouds clear; a brief sun, the winds die.
A wan streak of bilious light in the sky before dark,
'the attic study and the unfinished work'.
Only at dusk Athene's owl will fly,
only at dusk does wisdom return to the park.
On winter evenings, as the cars flash by,
what hides there in the kingdom of mould and bark?
Beyond the iron railings and the little gate
perhaps a fox stirs, and dead leaves conflate
in a dried-up fountain crisp-packet and matchbox,
the bright pavilion silent in its nook;
dead leaves up here too, lamplight night and day.
Commuters hustle home to Terenure and Foxrock
while I sit in the inner city with my book
— *Fanny Hill, À Rebours, The Picture of Dorian Gray* —
the pleasures of the text, periphrasis and paradox,
some languorous prose at odds with phone and fax.
The psychiatrist locks up and puts out the light
on desk and couch in his consulting rooms.
It's cold up here in the city of litter and drums
while fires glow in the hearths of suburban homes.
I have no peacocks, porphyries, prie-dieux,
no lilies, cephalotis, nepenthes, 'unnatural' vices,
yet I too toil not neither do I spin, I too
have my carefully constructed artificial paradises.
A foxy lady slips into her shoes
and leaves me words of wisdom; when she goes
I sit here like Domitian in a hecatomb of dead flies,
an armchair explorer in an era of cheap flight
diverted by posters, steamer and seaplane
at rest in tropical ports. I read where your man
transforms his kitchen into a quarterdeck

to simulate ocean travel and not get sick.
I get sea breezes in my own galley all right,
particularly before dawn when, war in heaven, I hear
remote winds rippling in the stratosphere
and regret never having visited Rio, Shanghai,
Haiti, Kyoto or the South Seas; though why
travel when imagination can get you there in a tick
and you're not plagued by the package crowd? A mature
artist takes the material closest to hand;
besides, in our post-modern world economy
one tourist site is much like another site
and the holy city comes down to a Zeno tour,
the closer you get the more it recedes from sight
and the more morons block your vision.
                                        Beyond
the backlit tree-tops of Fitzwilliam Square
a high window is showing one studious light,
somebody sitting late at a desk like me.
There are some diehards still on the upper floors,
a Byzantine privacy in mews and lane,
but mostly now the famous Georgian doors
will house a junk-film outfit or an advertising agency.
The fountain's flute is silent though time spares
the old beeches with their shades of Coole demesne;
inward investment conspires against old decency,
computer talks to computer, machine to answering machine.

3

At the Shelbourne

(Elizabeth Bowen, Nov., 1940)

Sunrise in the Irish Sea, dawn over Dublin Bay
after a stormy night, one shivering star;
and I picture the harsh waking everywhere,
the devastations of a world at war,
airfields, radio silence, a darkened convoy
strung out in moonlight on a glittering sea.
Harsh the wide windows of the hotel at daybreak
as I light up the first ciggie of the day,
stormy the lake like the one in Regent's Park,
glittering the first snow on the Wicklow hills.
Out back, a precipitous glimpse of silent walls,
courtyards, skylights of kitchen and heating plant,
seagulls in rising steam; while at the front
I stand at ease to hear the kettle sing
in an upper room of the Kildare St. wing,
admiring the frosty housetops of my birthplace
miraculously immune (almost) to bomb damage.
Sun through south-facing windows lights again
on the oval portrait and the polished surface
where, at an Empire writing table, I set down
my situation reports for the Dominions Office,
pen-sketches of MacEntee, James Dillon and the rest,
letters to friends in Cork or in Gower St.,
— Virginia, Rosamond and the *Horizon* set —
bright novelistic stuff, a nation on the page:
'. . . *deep, rather futile talks. It is hard afterwards*
to remember the drift, though I remember words,
that smoke-screen use of words! Mostly I meet
the political people; they are very religious.'

There's nothing heroic or 'patriotic' about this;
for here in this rentier heaven of racing chaps,
journalists, cipher clerks, even Abwehr types

and talkative day trippers down from Belfast,
I feel like a traitor spying on my own past.
It was here the ill-fate of cities happened first —
a cruiser in the Liffey, field guns trained on the GPO,
the kicking-in of doors, dances cancelled, revolvers
served with the morning tea on silver salvers,
a ghostly shipboard existence down below,
people asleep in corridors as now
in the London Underground, mysterious Kôr,
a change of uniforms in the cocktail bar
though the bronze slave girls still stand where they were,
Nubian in aspect, in manner art-nouveau.
This is home really, a place of warmth and light,
a house of artifice neither here nor there
between the patrician past and the egalitarian future,
tempting one always to prolong one's visit:
in war, peace, rain or fog you couldn't miss it
however late the hour, however dark the night.

4

'shiver in your tenement'

You might have thought them mature student, clerk
or priest once, long ago in the demure sixties
before the country first discovered sex —
Cathal O'Shannon, Harry Kernoff, Austin Clarke
arriving by bus at noon in search of roguery
from Howth, Raheny, Monkstown or Templeogue,
some house by bridge or woodland *à l'usage*
of the temporal, of the satiric or lyric Muse.
Gravely they strolled down Dawson or Grafton St.,
thoughtful figures amid the faces, the laughter,
or sat among the race-goers and scroungers
in Sinnott's, Neary's, the Bailey, the Wicklow Lounge —
pale, introspective almost to the point of blindness
or so it seemed, living the life of the mind,
of European *littérateurs*, their black Quartier hats
(all purchased from the same clerical outfitter)
suggestive of first editions and dusty attics.

They sipped watery Jameson — without ice, of course —
knew London and Paris but preferred the unforced
pace of the quiet city under the Dublin mountains
where a broadsheet or a broadcast might still count.
Those were the days before tourism and economic growth,
before deconstruction and the death of the author,
when pubs had as yet no pictures of Yeats and Joyce
since people could still recall their faces, their voices;
of crozier-wielding bishops, vigilant censors,
pre-conciliar Latin, smoke pouring from swung censers;
of sexual guilt, before French letter and Dutch cap,
fear muttered in the dark of dormitory and side chapel.
There was much dark then in the archdiocese
though some, like you, had found a gap of brightness —
now, of course, we live in a blaze of tropical light
under a green pagoda sunshade globally warm
like the slick glass on a renovated farmhouse.

Mnemosyne, mother of nine, dust at St Patrick's,
labour 'accustomed to higher living', poverty old hat,
does art benefit from the new dispensation?
What, in our new world, have we left to say?
Oh, poets can eat now, painters can buy paint
but have we nobler poetry, happier painting
than when the gutters bubbled, the drains stank
and hearts bobbed to the clappers in the sanctuary?
Has art, like life itself, its source in agony?
Nothing to lose but our chains, our chains gone
that bound with form the psycho-sexual turbulence,
together with those black hats and proper pubs,
at home now with the ersatz, the pop, the phoney,
we seldom love or hate, as once, with a full heart.
Those were the days; now patience, courage, artistry,
solitude things of the past, like the love of God,
we nod to you from the pastiche paradise of the post-modern.

5

Schopenhauer's Day

The recent past always presents itself as if destroyed by catastrophes.
— T. W. Adorno

What does the old bastard see when he looks down?
A creature of habit like everyone in this town,
he has lived up there above the promenade
for more than twenty years, and every day
observed the same deliberate formulae
now second nature: up at dawn, just one
mug of his favourite Java before work
— ethics — flute practice (K.299),
pan-pipes in honour of a previous life;
then lunch with students at the Englischer Hof
and reads till four, when he goes for the daily walk —
two hours, neither more nor less, hail, rain or shine.
At six to the library and a magazine,
a thicket of fiddle bows in the Kaisersaal,
a solitary supper at the Stork Hotel,
home by ten and early to bed: a routine
perfected over the years and one designed
to release from trivia the aspiring mind.
Cabs and coaches clash and squeal in the square,
the money-making craze is everywhere;
but a fire of pine or spruce keeps out the cold.
A pedestrian, mildly valetudinarian bachelor,
he stares from the window at his idea of the world,
its things-in-themselves, the sun rising once more
on bridge and embankment, baroque edifice, Gothic spire.

Minerals rage, base metals dreaming of gold
in the hills, while St Bartholomew chimes the hour;
plants, water, citizens, the very stone
expand with a sulphurous purpose of their own;
the very viruses scream to the higher forms.
Tat tvam asi; these living things we are

but only in the extinction of our desire,
absorption of the knower in the known.
There are perceptual difficulties, the *trompe-l'oeil*
of virtual reality; for what is real really?
Often we think what we see is not what we think we see;
he too is a mere appearance dreamt by another system,
he can't get through to the world nor the world to him.
As the Buddhists do, he tries to concentrate
on a faint chime, say, or on the idea of 'white'
while knowing these exercises cannot mitigate
life's guilt or the servitude of love and hate.
The only solution lies in *art for its own sake*,
redemption through the aesthetic, as birds in spring
sing for their own delight, even if they also sing
from physical need; it comes to the same thing.

   Bring out the poets and the artists; take
music, the panacea for all our woes,
the heartfelt calculus of Bach and Mozart
or the calm light of Dutch interior art;
and yet, he says, he fears for the fate of those
born in a later era, as if our bleak
and pitiless whoring after the sublime,
implying conflict as sublimity does,
bequeathed some frightfulness to a future time:
'Through the cortex a great melancholy blows
as if I'd seen the future in a dream —
Weimar, a foul Reich and the days of wrath,
a *Vogue* model in the dead dictator's bath;
and the angel of history, a receding plane
that leaves the cities a rubble of ash and bone
while GI Joe tap-dances on my gravestone.'

6

To Eugene Lambe in Heaven

— University Rd., Belfast, 1961; etc.

It's after closing time on a winter night
in Smoky Joe's café a generation ago —
rain and smoke, and the tables are packed tight
with drunken students kicking up a racket,
exchanging insults, looking for a fight
since there's nothing to do and nowhere else to go;
and the grave Italians (parents, daughter, son)
who own the place and serve these savages
of the harsh north their chips and sausages
look up and smile with relief as you come in,
their baffled faces lighting up at once
at your quaint 'whisker' and velvet smoking jacket,
your manner that of an exiled Stuart prince
transfiguring tedium . . . Next year you appeared
in the same gear and spread Tolstoyan beard,
our Ginger Man, in Trinity's front square
you called the 'playground' once; and it was here
in pub and flat you formed the character
we came to love, colloquial yet ornate,
one of those perfect writers who never write,
a student of manners and conversation straight
from the pages of Castiglione or Baudelaire:
'a form of pride rare in this generation,
stoical, spiritual even, resistant to the trite;
the Protestant countries lack gallantry and devotion . . . '

Not that you read much, you had no need to read
so flunked your courses; destined for the law
took up, instead, interior decoration,
installing yourself wherever the calling led
and awaiting the 'rush of gold' you never saw.
There you were, in the fine house of a friend,
a citrous gin or herbal tea to hand,

young women in attendance, an abashed host constrained
to listen patiently while you explained
the iniquity of ownership; for you had no ambition
save for the moment, of willpower not a whit
since nothing could measure up to your idea of it.
Dublin in the sixties — golden days
of folk revival, tin whistle and *bodhrán*,
ecology, yin and yang, CND, late-century blues,
Gandalf's Garden, *Bananas* and *Peace News*;
then London, Covent Garden, and quit the booze.
At a time of drag and pop art, hair and clothes,
Beardsley prints, floral design and rainbow hues,
of Biba, Hammond and Shrimpton, lurid tights,
commodity fetishism, instant celebrity, insolent pose,
yours was a sociable life but a lonely one,
your castle of indolence a monastic den
where you sat up late to contemplate the din
of Leicester Square, Long Acre and Drury Lane,
vocations entertained but never followed through.
A job, a house, a car, perhaps a wife,
financial panic, the 'normal' sort of life
so many know, such things were not for you
who made the great refusal but remained
philosophical with your dwindling flow of visitors,
chivalrous with women, ceremonious with waiters,
noble in exile, tragic in the end,
and died dancing . . . But hip went out of fashion
in an age of sado-monetarism, and the game
now is to the 'oeconomists and calculators' —
the new harshness must have wounded you to the heart.

We always knew you had too big a heart,
we always knew about the heart condition
you nursed with a vegetarian regime
of rice and nuts. You were a saint and hero
to the young men and girls we used to know
once in the golden age; and now it's closing time

in the condemned playgrounds that you loved, Eugene,
in Davy Byrne's and Smoky Joe's. The scene
is draggy now in these final days, and with
everyone famous for fifteen minutes, few
survive except those, like you, the stuff of myth.
Oft in the stilly night I remember our wasted youth.

7

An Bonnán Buí

A heron-like species, rare visitors, most recent records referring
to winter months . . . very active at dusk.
— A Field Guide to Irish Birds

A sobering thought, the idea of you stretched there,
bittern, under a dark sky, your exposed bones
yellow too in a ditch among cold stones,
ice glittering everywhere on bog and river,
the whole unfortunate country frozen over
and your voice stilled by enforced sobriety —
a thought more wrenching than the fall of Troy
because more intimate; for we'd hear your shout
of delight from a pale patch of watery sunlight
out on the mud there as you took your first
drink of the day and now, destroyed by thirst,
you lie in brambles while the rats rotate.
I'd've broken the ice for you, given an inkling;
now, had I known it, we might both be drinking
and singing too; for ours is the same story.
Others have perished — blackbird, finch, wren —
and lie shivering like you beneath hedge and whin;
but I mourn only the bittern, withdrawn and solitary,
who used to carouse alone among the rushes
and sleep rough in the star-glimmering bog drain.
It used to be, with characters like us,
they'd let us wander the roads in wind and rain
or lock us up and throw away the key —
but now they have a cure for these psychoses
as indeed they do for most social diseases
and, rich at last, we can forget our pain.
She says I'm done for if I drink again;
so now, relieved of dangerous stimuli,
at peace with my plastic bottle of H_2O
and the slack strings of insouciance, I sit
with bronze Kavanagh on his canal-bank seat,

not in 'the tremendous silence of mid-July'
but the fast bright zing of a winter afternoon
dizzy with headset, flash-bulb and digifone,
to learn the *tao* he once claimed as his own
and share with him the moorhen and the swan,
the thoughtless lyric of a cloud in the sky
and the play of light and shadow on the slow
commemorative waters; relax, go with the flow.

8

Hangover Square

The snowman infants from the nursery school
devised from the first fall of January
stares back from a far corner of the square —
a selfish giant made to freeze and rule
the garden as if self-generated there,
his abstract mien and cold, bituminous eye
proclaiming a different order of reality
from the bright children who gave rise to him.
When they go there to play at mid-morning
their primary colours seem to prefigure spring,
the deliquescence of each rigorous thing;
but the ex-child at the window watching them,
specs on his nose and winter in his eyes,
knows himself outcast from the continuum
and draws his curtain against darkening skies . . .
A long time since the hearties and the aesthetes,
imperious questors and saint-faced degenerates,
old boys of Yeats's 'tragic generation'
in cricketing blazers and inept bow ties
who ate the altar rails, pawned pride for drinks
or tumbled from high stools in the Rose & Crown.
Those desperate characters of the previous nineties,
slaves of the Siren, consorts of the Sphinx
like Dowson, Johnson, Symons and Le Gallienne
were heroes, though, compared with our protagonist,
a decadent who lived to tell the story,
surviving even beyond the age of irony
to the point where the old stuff comes round again;
and this is the sin against the Holy Ghost,
the cynicism that views with equanimity
the enemies of promise, *les amours jaunes*,
the organism dark with booze and nicotine.
Today is the first day of the rest of your life?
— tell that to your liver; tell that to your ex-wife.

Owning like them 'an indolent, restless gift',
fitful, factitious and at best makeshift,
burning without warmth or illumination,
each verse co-terminous with its occasion,
each line the pretext for a precious cadence,
I keep alight the cold candle of decadence.
A rueful veteran of the gender wars,
in 'the star-crowned solitude of oblivious hours'
I remember London twilights blue with gin
sub regno Cynarae, the wine and roses
where 'She-who-must-be-obeyed', furs next the skin,
drove us to celibacy or satyriasis.
'Nothing, of course, not even conventional virtue
is so provincial as conventional vice'
— Symons, *The Symbolist Movement in Literature*.
The most of what we did and wrote was artifice,
rhyme-sculpture against the entangling vines of nature —
a futile project since, in the known future,
real books will be rarities in techno culture,
a forest of intertextuality like this,
each one a rare book and what few we have
written for prize money and not for love.
No doubt I should invest in a computer
but I'm sticking with my old electric typewriter,
its thick click, black ink on the white pages,
one letter at a time, fuzz round the edges.

9

At the Gate Theatre

(*for Dearbhla Molloy*)

'. . . Ah, what new pain must I now undergo?
What monstrous torture have I yet to know?
All I've endured, the madness and the fear,
self-pity, rage, humiliation, self-hate,
the insult of rejection, even, were mere
ripples of the approaching storm . . . ' Not many
in the trade now can decently impersonate
the great ones of the tragic repertoire
— Medea, Cleopatra, Lady Macbeth —
much less achieve the famous 'diamond edge'
of the doomed Phaedra's lightning-inviting rage,
her great apostrophes to love and death;
so here am I, like any stage-door Johnny,
to call your playing out of Phaedra's agony,
your bright contralto, stringed and starlit vertigo
of outrage and despair from head to toe
not only wonderful but actually sublime
in the old sense of resistance overcome,
articulate terror, storm answered with storm,
a heaven-splitting performance. When she cries
defiance to the gods, the wings, the quivering flies,
we know we are in the presence; but we know too
a whole theatrical tradition is in crisis —
this play peaked and exhausted all at once
an entire genre; for its fierce eloquence
yielded in no time to the *comic* Muse,
the death of tragedy and the Birth of the Blues.
Backstage tonight, I glimpse the ghostly faces
of Micheál and Hilton, Geraldine and Siobhán
amid the festive racket of make-up and paint-sprays,
Hedda Gabler, The School for Scandal, Happy Days,
moonlit revels and laughter in the dark,
the thrill of envenom'd chalice and poisonous book;

for tragedy too, of course, is enormous fun
though now we've no use for the tragic posture.
The Greeks mixed tragedies with satyr plays;
and look at the old age of Euripides
who, after a lifetime struggling with new ideas,
sends out his Bacchae to the woods and glens
to dance devotion to the god of vines
under the rocks, under the moonlit pines,
for Dionysus, son of Semele, is come.
Bring on ivy and goatskin, pipe and drum!

11

At the Chelsea Arts Club

Everything aspires to the condition of pop music,
the white noise of late-century consumerism —
even Whistler's Thames, once 'clothed in evening mist
where the buildings lose themselves in a dim sky,
the great chimneys become campanili
and warehouses are palaces in the night'.
Now both embankments gleam with exhausted chrome
revving at funeral pace, with the home team
up in the league and quoted on the exchange
and interest in the game at fever pitch,
we treasure the more those symphonies in white,
those nocturnes consecrating wharf and bridge.
Elsewhere the body art, snuff sculpture, trash aesthetics,
the video nasties and shock computer graphics;
but here you still might meet with 'significant form' —
indeed, the interior illustrates the term
with its retro mode and snooker table, piano,
'the whole place rather like a studio',
shirts by Jekyll & Hyde, the wine and roses,
the sniftery dandies at their studied poses,
the eyepatch woman and the monocle man,
Caroline and Justine, Georgina, Fanny,
Abercrombie & Fitch, Savile Row, Armani,
garden and sky rose-red and Dufy-blue.
Maybe I'm finally turning into an old fart
but I do prefer the traditional kinds of art,
respect for materials, draughtsmanship and so on —
though I'm in two minds about Tank Girl over there,
the Muse in chains, a screw bolt in one ear,
the knickers worn over the biking gear . . .

Best in the afternoon when the bar is shut,
the smoking room, an empty Chekhov set,
stained ochre, yields to silence, buttery light,
euphoria and nostalgia; so let me write

in praise of yellow while it is still bright —
of crocus and freesia, primrose and daffodil,
the novels of Huxley, Rimbaud's missing vowel,
yahoos, yippies, yuppies, yoga, yoghurt, Yale,
bananas, Danaë's golden shower, baby clothes and toys,
prohibition, quarantine, caution, cowardice, buoys,
lamplight, gaslight, candlelight, illness, fog,
pencils, *I Ching*, golf, 'radio-active', bubonic plague,
illuminated scripture, Klimt and Schiele, Kafka's Prague,
Aladdin's lamp and genie, mechanical earth-movers,
treason, deceit, infection, misery, unhappy lovers,
a night wake, magic realism, Gnosticism, Cabbalism,
guilt and grief, conspiracy theories, crime,
the back pages, dangerous liaisons, journalism,
charity, sunlit smoke, delight and shame,
angels and archangels, cherubim and seraphim,
the earliest buses, the Congo, Manhattan taxis,
cottage doors, the old *telefón* boxes,
failure, the word 'curious', the word 'screech'
and the little patch of brick Proust liked so much.

12

Aphrodite's Pool

I dive and rise in an explosion of spindrift
and drift to a turtle-faced inflatable raft —
evening, Cyclades, one cloud in the azure,
a brain-scan light show swarming on blue tiles,
a flickering network of vague energies
as on dolphin murals and docked caique bows,
a murmuring hosepipe where the pool fills,
snatches of music from a quiet house,
the pump room like a temple to the Muses;
on a marble slab flipper and apple core,
straw hat and wristwatch in a deckchair,
sandal and white sock. Nymphs have been here;
water nymphs have been here printing the blind
nap-time silence with supernatural toes
and casting magic on the sparkling water
still agitated by a dry seasonal wind.
Donkeys chew the roses, swifts skim the ripples,
a last plane fades beyond the glittering sound,
its wild surfboards and somnolent fishing boats,
as the air fills with cicadas and mosquitoes,
the sky with sunset and astronomy; goats
and ravens nod in the god-familiar hills
among spaceship vertebrae and white asphodels.

Aloof from the disco ships and buzzing bikes
the pool ticks faintly among quiet rocks;
soft petals on the surface and in the air,
mimosa and jasmine fragrance everywhere,
I flirt like some corrupt, capricious emperor
with insects dithering on the rim; for this
is the mythic moment of metamorphosis
when quantitative becomes qualitative and genes
perform their atom-dance of mad mutation . . .
I climb out, shower off chlorine and sun lotion,
and a hot turquoise underwater light

glows like Atlantis in the Aegean night;
network, stars-of-the-sea, perpetual motion,
a star-net hums in the aphrodisiac sea lanes.

14

Rue des Beaux Arts

There is only one thing . . . worse than being talked about,
and that is not being talked about.
> — Oscar Wilde

The new art is everywhere with its whiplash line
derived from pre-Raff ivy and twining vine,
its biomorphic shapes, motifs of cat and moth;
base metals and industrial design,
outside and inside, in themselves uncouth,
aspire to the carnal life of pond and bower —
and you yourself, old trendy that you are,
have exchanged the silvery tinkle of champagne
for muddy clouds of absinthe and vermouth,
bitter herbs self-prescribed to make you whole.
As you said, a yellow-journalism survivor
has no need to fear the yellow fever;
but it's mid-July and nature has crept back
to the rue des Beaux Arts and the rue du Bac,
the humid side streets of the Latin Quarter
with its rank plants and warm municipal water,
its fiery pavements scorching feet and soul;
'the whole body gives out a silent scream'.
Deep in the silent pharmacy of your room
you doze most of the day with curtains drawn
against the hot-house light of afternoon,
rising at agate Paris dusk to take
your walk by the twilit river, *quai des brumes*,
and check with the sales people at Galignani's
on the latest magazines; and more than once
you've mixed with tourists in the Luxembourg
to watch schoolchildren under the stony gaze
of Anne de Bretagne and Marguerite de Provence
and listen to infants piping in the Coupole,
your Babylonian features raised in reminiscence.
'Art's mainspring, the love of life, is gone;

prose is so much more difficult.' The morgue
yawns, as it yawned too for Verlaine, Laforgue,
nor will you see your wife and sons again.
Gestures, a broken series; performance strain;
judge by appearances and what you get
is an old windbag. Still full of hot air,
still queer as fuck and putting on the style,
you spout in the Odéon given half a chance
for yours is the nonchalance of complete despair.
'*The thing now is to forget him; let him go*
to that limbo of oblivion which is his due' —
though the *Daily Chronicle* and the *St James Gazette*
are gone, while you are talked of even yet.

　　Backlit by sunset, a great trench of sky
glows like a brazier; grotesque tableaux,
unprecedented creatures are printed there
in angelic purple-and-gold photography
and the stars shine like gaslight. Gazing west
you can just make out the tip of Finistère
where the last rock explodes in glistening mist.
'*They will not want me again in airy mood;*
they would like me to edit prayers for those at sea.'
Job with a skin rash and an infected ear,
Oisín in the real world of enforced humility,
you pine still for the right kind of solitude
and the right kind of society; but it's too late
to benefit from the astringency of the sea
or come to terms with the nature you pooh-poohed;
for you, if anyone, have played your part
constraining nature in the name of art,
surviving long enough for the birth-knell
of a new century and a different world.
Go sup with the dead, the party's life and soul:
'*The greatest men fail, or seem to have failed.*'

15

Smoke

Bone idle, I lie listening to the rain,
not tragic now nor yet 'to frenzy bold' —
must I stand out in thunder yet again
who have *thrice* come in from the cold? Sold
on sobriety, I turn to the idea of nicotine,
my opium, hashish, morphine and cocaine.
Autumn in Dublin; safe home from New York
I climb as directed to our proper dark,
five flights without a lift up to the old
gloom we used to love, and the old cold.
Head in the clouds but tired of verse, I fold
away my wind-harp and my dejection odes
and mute the volume on the answerphone
('. . . leave your number; speak after the tone')
to concentrate on pipe dreams and smoke clouds.
Skywards smoke from my last Camel rises
as elsewhere from our natural resources
and the contagious bonfire of the vanities
like pillars of cloud. I was with Xenophon
in Persia, I was with the navigators
when first they landed on American shores
in search of a trade route to the Orient
and found instead, to their bewilderment,
a sot-weed continent in the western ocean.
Now closing time and the usual commotion,
crowds and cars as if to a revolution.
Geared up by Klein and Nike, Banana Republic, Gap,
we are all tourists now and there is no escape;
smoke gets in your face, in your eyes, up your nose
but offers inspiration, aspiration, hope,
lateral thinking, 'pure speculative ether',
an apolitical sphere above the weather.
26. *INT. RICK'S. A night-club, expensive, chic*
with an air of sophistication and intrigue
and everybody puffing; those were the days

of legendary nuance, 'drift', lavender haze.
No puffing now, not even on death row,
even in the electric chair tobacco is taboo.
. . . What *use* is it, you ask, as we exhale
clouds of unknowing with our last gasp. Well,
it suggests alternatives to the world we know
and is to that extent consoling; also
'a man should have an occupation of some kind'.
Raleigh, for instance, spent his time in Youghal
weighing cigars against cigar ashes to find
the weight of smoke, perhaps even of the soul;
and Bakhtin under siege, no soap, no supper,
used his own manuscripts as cigarette paper.

16

America Deserta

High in the air float green-blue copper roofs like the tips of castles
rising from the clouds in fairy tales and cigarette advertisements.
                    — Zelda Fitzgerald, *Harper's Bazaar,* 1929

Often enough you've listened to me complain
of the routine sunshine and infrequent rain
beyond the ocean blue; and now, begod,
where once it never drizzled but it poured,
in dirty Dublin and even in grim Belfast
our cherished rainfall is a thing of the past,
our climate now that of the world at large
in the post-Cold War, global-warming age
of corporate rule, McPeace and Mickey Mao.
Imitative in all things, we mimic now,
as nature art, the general New Age weather.
Anxious not to be left behind, we seize
on the dumb theory and the prescribed disease
who were known once for witty independence
and valued things beyond the world of sense;
subscribing eagerly to the post-modern kitsch
we shirk our noble birthright as the glitch
in the internet, the thorn in the side, the pain
in the neck and the holy ghost in the machine.
An alien among aliens during my New York time
spying for the old world in the new, thought crime
grown secretly like a window box of cannabis
in the shocking privacy of a book-lined space,
I valued above all our restful evening walks
to the West Side pierheads and the desolate docks.

    Back home now with my 20th-century blues
I surf the radiant icon for world news
and watch with sanctimonious European eyes
Get Real, Global Impact, Born to Kill.
Not long from barbarism to decadence, not far

from liberal republic to defoliant empire
and thence to entropy; not long before
the great money scam begins its long decline
to pot-holed roads and unfinished construction sites,
as in the dark ages a few scattered lights —
though it's only right and proper we set down
that in our time New York was a lot of fun.
I think of diner mornings in ice and thaw,
the Lion's Head, renamed the Monkey's Paw,
you wildly decadent in forbidden furs
in the shadow of the Bobst or the Twin Towers,
the skyline at your back, the pearl-rope bridges
and a nation singing its heart out in the yellow pages.

17

The World of J. G. Farrell

(*for Lavinia Greacen*)

A huge house (*Troubles*) at the water's edge
whistling and groaning in the wind from the sea,
blind windows, flying slates, whole days of reverie,
'the cemetery of all initiative and endeavour',
outbuildings, tea-gold streams, a heathery road
where the hero comes to claim his dying bride,
a primrose vintage 'motor' in the garage,
crows bickering high up in a foggy wood,
vegetable encroachments, intestinal shapes,
the click and ripple of exhausted pipes,
a creeper twining around a naked light
while a young man, inspected by binoculars,
harangues a restive crowd from a watery rock;
hill stations deserted (*Siege*), impenetrable foliage,
long bars empty (*Grip*) in tropical heat,
pools afloat with matchboxes and driftwood,
flyblown verandahs, ceiling fans at rest,
carnivorous plants entangling gates and fences,
the coercive empire an empire of the senses,
of rustling organisms and whispering rain forest,
a dripping silence after torrential rain,
the fluttering butterfly that starts the hurricane.

Better a quiet life, the moon in a bucket of water
with nobody there to hear though the stars do
and a bedside book like the teachings of Chuang Tzu —
type of the unselfconscious thinker who,
never a slave to objective reality, knew
our vital unity with the rest of nature;
disdained, of course, utilitarian method;
like Echo, answered only when called upon
in bamboo cage or palace of white jade.
We have lost our equilibrium, he said;

gaze at the world but leave the world alone.
Do nothing; do nothing and everything will be done.

18

A Bangor Requiem

We stand — not many of us — in a new cemetery
on a cold hillside in the north of Co. Down
and stare at an open grave or out to sea,
the lough half-hidden by great drifts of rain.
Only a few months since you were snug at home
in a bungalow glow, keeping provincial time
in the chimney corner, *News-Letter* and *Woman's Own*
on your knee, wool-gathering by Plato's firelight,
a grudging flicker of flame on anthracite.
Inactive since your husband died, your chief
concern the 'appearances' that ruled your life
in a neighbourhood of bay windows and stiff
gardens shivering in the salt sea air,
the sunburst ideogram on door and gate,
you knew the secret history of needlework,
bread-bin and laundry basket awash with light,
the straight-backed chairs, the madly chiming clock.
The figure in the *Republic* returns to the cave,
a Dutch interior where cloud shadows move,
to examine the intimate spaces, chest and drawer,
the lavender in the linen, the savings book,
the kitchen table silent with nobody there.
Shall we say the patience of an angel? No,
not unless angels be thought anxious too.
God knows you had reason to be; and yet
with your wise monkeys and 'Dresden' figurines,
your junk chinoiserie and coy pastoral scenes,
you too were an artist, a rage-for-order freak
setting against a man's aesthetic of cars and golf
your ornaments and other breakable stuff.
Visible from your window the 6th-century
abbey church of Colum and Malachi,
'light of the world' once in the monastic ages,
home of antiphonary and the golden pages
of radiant scripture; though you had your own

idea of the beautiful, not unrelated to Tolstoy
but formed in a tough city of ships and linen,
Harland & Wolff, Mackie's, Gallaher's, Lyle & Kinahan
and your own York St. Flax Spinning Co. Ltd.;
daft musicals at the Curzon and the Savoy.

   Beneath a Castilian sky, at a great mystic's rococo tomb,
I thought of the plain Protestant fatalism of home.
Remember 1690; prepare to meet thy God —
I grew up among washing lines and grey skies,
pictures of Brookeborough on the gable ends,
revolvers, RUC, 'B' Specials, law-'n'-order,
a hum of drums above the summer glens
shattering the twilight over lough water
in a violent post-industrial sunset blaze
while you innocently hummed 'South of the Border',
'On a Slow Boat to China', 'Beyond the Blue Horizon'.
Little soul, the body's guest and companion,
this is a cold epitaph from your only son,
the wish genuine if the tone ambiguous.
Oh, I can love you now that you're dead and gone
to the many mansions in your mother's house;
all artifice stripped away, we give you back to nature
but something of you, perhaps the incurable ache
of art, goes with me as I travel south
past misty drumlins, shining lanes to the shore,
above the Mournes a final helicopter,
sun-showers and rainbows all the way through Louth,
cottages buried deep in ivy and rhododendron,
ranch houses, dusty palms, blue skies of the republic . . .

19

Christmas in Kinsale

After the fairy lights in seaside lounge and bar
the night walk under a blustery Advent sky,
sidereal frost systems money will never buy,
one gull on a night wave, one polished star,
crane light at the quayside, a dark harbour mouth.
Wind chimes this morning through dispersing mist
from the Church of Ireland and St John the Baptist,
smoke rising like incense from a chimney pot.
Once, angels on every branch, scribes in the trees,
'a continuous chorus of divine praise'.
Does history, exhausted, come full circle?
It ended here at a previous *fin de siècle*
though leaving vestiges of a distant past
before Elizabeth and the Tudor conquest —
since when, four hundred years of solitude,
rain on crushed bluebells in an autumn wood . . .

Holed up here in the cold gardens of the west
I take out at mid-morning the Christmas rubbish.
Sphere music, the morning stars consort together
in a fine blaze of anticyclone weather
cradling the calm inner, the rough outer harbour,
the silence of frost and crow on telephone lines,
the wet and dry, the cardboard and the trash,
remains of rib and chop, warm cinders, ash,
bags, boxes, bulbs and batteries, bathroom waste,
paper and tinfoil, leaves, crumbs, scraps and bones —
if this were summer there would be clouds of flies
buzzing for joy around the rubbish bins.

The harsh will dies here among snails and peonies,
its grave an iridescence in the sea breeze,
a bucket of water where the rainbow ends.
Elsewhere the cutting edge, the tough cities,
the nuclear wind from Windscale, derelict zones;

here the triumph of carnival, rinds and skins,
mud-wrestling organisms in post-historical phase
and the fuzzy vegetable glow of origins.
A cock crows good-morning from an oil drum
like a peacock on a rain-barrel in Byzantium;
soap-bubbles foam in a drainpipe and life begins.
I dreamed last night of a blue Cycladic dawn,
again the white islands shouting, 'Come on; come on!' . . .

Quaderno

1 AN ICE-CREAM AT CAPRONI'S
— Bangor, 1939

She sits there tinkering with an ice-cream
of many colours, lost in a private dream;
she wears a hat, gloves and a frilly blouse
and shivers slightly in a summer breeze:
if only time could stop like this before
life choices, childbirth and the coming war.

2 BEYOND THE ALPS

He slopes off into the snow without his skis.
Gudrun sees him vanish: what can she do
as he goes ghost-like under lowering skies?
Blind hut, dim crucifix, while far below
the inn lights and the old imperial road
point to the happier lives they might have led.

3 CASA SUL MARE

A sheet of morning mist and a light breeze
lull self-effacing waves and cavities.
No sparkling breakers and no flying foam;
but it still waits for you, that little room
in this remembering house, your hands and eyes
plumping the pillows, making yourself at home.

4 DIOGENES ON THE SHORE

I want no strangers standing in my light,
their hearts at peace, and I deplore the sight
of tedious tourists with their cine-cameras
spoiling our quiet vistas and panoramas.

We spend our days conversing with chimeras
and take a torch when we go out at night.

5 GERONIMO

'Geronimo!', I thought, when an Etruscan
appeared in a drowsy garage at Cerveteri.
He had the earthy look of primitive man,
carried himself like a spry veteran
of tribal conflict, disinherited yet
blithe, and took off in an ancient Fiat.

6 PASOLINI

Cruising for wild *ragazzi* out of season,
he sat late at Giordano's and drove down
in his Alfa Romeo to the seaplane basin
where, knifed and mangled in the sand and ash,
a wreck but recognizable, he lives on
as a bronze bird-shape shining amid the trash.

7 I PENSIEROSI

We too spent time in the high lonely tower,
bricks and bridges fading from rose to grey,
the anglepoise tilted at midnight hour
with other lamps aglow in Fiesole,
a silent fountain and an ivy hedge
reflecting the grave thoughts of middle age.

8 PAOLO AND LIGHEA

A young man slept with a mermaid one fine night
in the blue depths of an Ischian sea-cave
where 'she ate nothing that was not alive',
and nothing since has ever been quite right.
He lives alone now, unlike you and me,
his briny heart nostalgic for the sea.

9 BEATRICE HASTINGS

'I retain only memories and pictures,
stirring and palpable, perhaps overdone
in homage to your most endearing features;
also your verses, dance routines and one
or two love phrases, intimate and funny,
murmured to your admirer, Modigliani.'

10 '. . . DOVE PER SOLE . . .'
— *Dino Campana*

I loved you in a city where the solitary
step rings in an empty thoroughfare
eirenic dusk relieves with a rain shower
and the incorrigible heart once more
turns to an ambiguous spring in violet
distances beyond the washed-out sky.

High Water

Starved for pedestrian silence and in flight
from the 'totality and simultaneity' of data,
we stand on the Gesuati steps at high water
inhaling the rain-rinsed air of the Zattere.
Year-round tourism now, a perpetual high tide,
bright shadow of the present on old souls;
though still in a cool corner we can hide
with morning sunbeams at the swirling tiles,
a bracing sea-stench from the rotting piles,
hump bridges, monks, and girls with parasols.
A paper moon dissolves in cloud canals,
the colours fading as they come to light.

Ghosts

We live the lives our parents never knew
when they sang 'Come Back to Sorrento'.
Driving west in the evening from Pompeii,
its little houses sealed up in a tomb
of ash and pumice centuries ago
and now exposed to the clear light of day,
we found an old hotel with a sea view
and Naples' lights reflected in the bay
where, with a squeal of seagulls far below,
white curtains blew like ghosts into the room.

Head

What I hold, life size, is the near-final
revelation of form, a moulded head inclined
to an absorbing task, some job in hand.
Running my fingers round from the spinal
bump of the skull to the shut lip and eye
I wait for it to give tongue, to avail
of language; and it does, but silently,
its thought enclosed in that intent oval.

Words come to a head and fail, but faces win —
artful inflections of the giving skin
stretched over the tense wiring of desire.
She lies there at an angle, the work done,
inert but wide awake, the watchful brain
at rest, once more preparing to inspire.

Roman Script

Nei rifiuti del mondo nasce un nuovo mondo.

— Pasolini

I

Rain in the night; now cock-crow and engine hum
wake us at first light on the Janiculum
and we open the shutters to extravagant mists
behind which an autumn sun hotly insists:
parasol pine, low dove and glistening drop,
bright lemon, jonquil, jasmine and heliotrope —
the Respighi moment, life mimicking art again
as when the fiddles provoke line-dancing rain.

2

Turn back into the room where sunlight shows
dim ceilings, domino tiles, baroque frescoes,
a scenic interior, a theatrical space
for Byronic masquerade or Goldoni farce,
vapours and swordsmanship, the cape and fan,
the amorous bad-boy and the glamorous nun,
boudoir philosophy, night music on balconies,
the gondola section nodding as in a sea breeze.

3

Rome of conspiracy theories and lost causes,
exiles have died here in your haunted palaces
where our own princes, flushed with wine and hope,
they say, and the squeal of a lone bagpipe
torn from the wild and windy western ocean,
dreamed up elaborate schemes of restoration —
a world more distant now than Pompeiian times
with the shipyards visible from the nymphaeums.

4

Type up the new stuff, nap between four and five
when for a second time you come alive
with flies that linger in November light
and moths not even camphor puts to flight;
listen with them to sepia furniture
and piano practice from the flat next door;
watch where the poplar spires of evening thin
to smoke-stains on the ochreous travertine.

5

Now out you go among the *botteghe oscure*
and fluttering street lamps of Trastevere,
over the bridge where Fiat and Maserati
burn up the racetrack of the eternal city,
floodlit naiad and triton; for at this hour
the beautiful and damned are in Harry's Bar
or setting out for pit stops, sexy dives
and parties, as in the movie of our lives.

6

Here they are, Nero, Julia, Poppaea, Diocletian
and the shrewd popes of a later dispensation
at ease in bath-house and in Coliseum
or raping young ones in the venial gym —
as the prophet said, as good a place as any
to watch the end of the world; to watch, at least,
the late mutation of the romantic egotist
when the knock comes at last for Don Giovanni.

7

Snap out of your art fatigue and take a trip
to church and basilica, forum, fountain and frieze,
to the Sistine Chapel's violent comic strip
or the soft marble thighs of Persephone; seize
real presence, the art-historical sublime,
in an intricate owl-blink Nikon moment of time,
in a flash-photography lightning storm above
Cecilia's actual body, Endymion's actual grave.

8

Mid-morning noise of prisoners playing hard
in the Regina Coeli's echoing exercise yard —
for even the wretched of the earth are here
with instructions to entertain the visitor;
and we walk in reality, framed as virtuality,
as in a film set, Cinecittà, a cinema city
where life is a waking dream in broad daylight
and everything is scripted for our delight.

9

Others were here, *comunque*, who dreamed in youth
of a society based on hope and faith —
the poet of internment, solitude, morning sea,
of the lost years when we used to fall in love
not with women themselves but some commodity,
a hat, a pair of shoes, a blouse, a glove
(to him death came with the eyes of a new age,
a facile cynicism restyled as image);

10

and the poet of poverty, ash on the night wind,
starlight and tower blocks on waste ground,
peripheral rubbish dumps beyond the noise
of a circus, where sedated girls and boys
put out for a few bob on some building site
in the cloudy imperium of ancient night
and in the ruins, amid disconsolate lives
on the edge of the artful city, a myth survives.

11

His is the true direction we have lost
since his corpse showed up on the beach at Ostia
and life as we know it evolved into imagery,
production values and revised history,
the genocidal corporate imperative
and the bright garbage on the incoming wave
best seen at morning rush hour in driving rain:
'in the refuse of the world a new world is born'.

Shapes and Shadows

— William Scott, oil on canvas,
Ulster Museum

The kitchens would grow bright
in blue frames; outside, still
harbour and silent cottages
from a time of shortages,
shapes deft and tranquil,
black kettle and black pot.

Too much the known structures
those simple manufactures,
communion of frying pans,
skinny beans and spoons,
colander and fish slice
in a polished interior space.

But tension of hand and heart
abstracted the growing art
to a dissonant design
and a rich dream of paint,
on the grim basic plan
a varied white pigment

knifed and scrubbed, in one
corner a boiling brown
study in mahogany;
beige-biscuit left; right
a fat patch of white,
bread and milk in agony.

Rough brushwork here, thick
but vague; for already
behind these there loom
shades of the prehistoric,
ghosts of colour and form,
furniture, function, body —

as if to anounce the death
of preconception and myth
and start again on the fresh
first morning of the world
with snow, ash, whitewash,
limestone, mother-of-pearl,

bleach, paper, soap, foam
and cold kitchen cream,
to find in the nitty-gritty
of surfaces and utensils
the shadow of a presence,
a long-sought community.

A Swim in Co. Wicklow

The only reality is the perpetual flow of vital energy.
— Montale

Spindrift, crustacean patience
and a gust of ozone,
you come back once more
to this dazzling shore,
its warm uterine rinse,
heart-racing heave and groan.

A quick gasp as you slip
into the hissing wash,
star cluster, dulse and kelp,
slick algae, spittle, froth,
the intimate slash and dash,
hard-packed in the seething broth.

Soft water-lip, soft hand,
close tug of origin,
the sensual writhe and snore
of maidenhair and frond,
you swim here once more
smart as a rogue gene.

Spirits of lake, river
and woodland pond preside
mildly in water never
troubled by wind or tide;
and the quiet suburban pool
is only for the fearful —

no wind-wave energies
where no sea briar grips
and no freak breaker with
the violence of the ages
comes foaming at the mouth
to drown you in its depths.

Among pebbles a white conch
worn by the suck and crunch,
a sandy skull as old
as the centuries, in cold
and solitude reclines
where the moon-magnet shines;

but today you swirl and spin
in sea water as if,
creatures of salt and slime
and naked under the sun,
life were a waking dream
and this the only life.

The Dream Play

What night-rule now about this haunted grove?

The spirits have dispersed, the woods
faded to grey from midnight blue
leaving a powdery residue,
night music fainter, frivolous gods
withdrawing, cries of yin and yang,
amid the branches a torn wing.

So what is this enchanted place?
Not the strict groves of academe
but an old thicket of lost time
and constant flux, recovered space
where the brain yields to nose and ear,
dawn silence of the biosphere,

and a dazed donkey, starry-eyed,
beside her naked nibs is laid.
Wild strains and viruses are here,
the electric moth touch of desire
and a new vision, a new regime
of yellow moonlight, dance and dream

induced by what mind-altering drug
or rough-cast magic realism —
till morning bright with ant and bug
shines in a mist of glistening gism,
shifting identities, mutant forms,
angels evolved from snails and worms.

St Patrick's Day

No wise man ever wished to be younger.
— Swift

1

Down the long library each marble bust
shines unregarded through a shower of dust
where a grim ghost paces for exercise
in wet weather: nausea, gout, 'some days
I hardly think it worth my time to rise'.
Not even the love of friends can quite appease
the vertigo, sore ears and inner voices;
deep-draughted rain clouds, a rock lost in space,
yahoos triumphant in the marketplace,
the isle is full of intolerable noises.

2

Go with the flow; no, going against the grain
he sits in his rocking chair with a migraine,
a light in the church all day till evensong,
the sort of day in which a man might hang.
No riding out to bubbling stream and weir,
to the moist meadow and white belvedere;
on tattling club and coffee house a pox,
a confederacy of dunces and mohocks —
scholars and saints be d-mn'd, slaves to a hard
reign and our own miniature self-regard.

3

We emerge from hibernation to ghetto-blasters
much better than our old Sony transistors,
consensual media, permanent celebration,
share options, electronic animation,

wave motion of site-specific daffodils,
closed-circuit video in the new hotels;
for Niamh and Oisín have come to earth once more
with blinding breastplate and tempestuous hair,
new festive orthodoxy and ironic icon,
their faces lit up like the Book of Kells.

4

Defrosting the goose-skin on Bridget's daughters
spring sunlight sparkles among parking meters,
wizards on stilts, witches on circus bikes,
jokers and jugglers, twitching plastic snakes,
pop music of what happens, throbbing skies,
star wars, designer genes, sword sorceries.
We've no nostalgia for the patristic croziers,
fridges and tumble-dryers of former years,
rain-spattered cameras in O'Connell St.,
the sound mikes buffeted by wind and sleet —

5

but this is your birthday and I want to recall
a first-floor balcony under a shower of hail
where our own rowdy crowd stood to review
post-Christian gays cavorting up Fifth Avenue,
wise-cracking dialogue as quick and dry
as that in *The Big Sleep* or *The Long Goodbye*;
for we too had our season in Tír na nÓg,
a Sacred Heart girl and a Protestant rogue,
chill sunshine warming us to the very bone,
our whole existence one erogenous zone.

6

I could resign these structures and devices,
these fancy flourishes and funny voices
to a post-literate, audio-visual realm
of uncial fluorescence, song and film,
as curious symptoms of a weird transition
before we opted to be slaves of fashion —
for now, whatever the ancestral dream,
we give ourselves to a vast corporate scheme
where our true wit is devalued once again,
our solitude known only to the rain.

7

The one reality is the perpetual flow,
chaos of complex systems. Each generation
does what it must; middle age and misanthropy,
like famine and religion, make poor copy,
and even the present vanishes like snow
off a rope, frost off a ditch, ice in the sun —
so back to the desktop and the drawing board,
prismatic natural light, slow-moving cloud,
the waves far-thundering in a life of their own,
a young woman hitching a lift on a country road.

Resistance Days

Nous nous aimerons tous et nos enfants riront
De la légende noire où pleure un solitaire.
— Paul Éluard

(*for John Minihan*)

The sort of snail mail that can take a week
but suits my method, pre-*informatique*,
I write this from the Louisiane, rm. 14 —
or type it, rather, on the old machine,
a portable, that I take when I migrate
in 'the run-up to Christmas'. Here I sit
amidst the hubbub of the rue de Seine
while a winter fly hums at a windowpane.
Old existentialists, old beats, old punks
sat here of old; some dedicated drunks
still sing in the marketplace, and out the back
there's an old guy who knew Jack Kerouac.
Spring in December now, of course: no doubt
the daffs and daisies are already out
and you lot, in the serene post-Christmas lull,
biking the back roads between Hob and Schull.
Here at the *heure bleue* in the Deux Magots
where as a student I couldn't afford to go,
a gauche and unregenerate anglophone
tongue-tied as ever in my foreign tongue,
still getting the easiest constructions wrong,
I inhale the fashions of the sexy city,
its streets streaming with electricity,
its swings and roundabouts on the go as ever,
the fly-boats echoing on the floodlit river
when a switch locks and the long boulevard flares
with a thump and flow obscuring moon and stars.

In flight from corporate Christendom, this year
I spent the frightful season in Tangier
with spaced-out 'fiscal nomads' and ex-pats

or bored by Bowles beneath the sheltering slats,
bucket and spade under high cloud and sail,
blue and windblown, a sort of vast Kinsale
— a travel poster as we fluttered down
changing at Casablanca in pouring rain;
then ocean contours, minaret and souq,
a dribbling fountain, swirling palms, wind sock,
a postcard; camels on the beach, black sheep
routinely scattering on the tiny strip,
the flowing script of Royal Air Maroc;
prescribed odours of cedarwood and kif
in the moist oasis of the Hotel du Rif,
swifts diving over the gardens and the port
of course, for even there the birds migrate;
heat-lightning flash photography in the strait,
eight lengths of a cold pool above a white
city at sea; keen carols on Christmas Day
with a lost tribe of Nigerian *sans-papiers*,
bright migrants from hot Sahara to cold EU
in the leafy English church Sam Beckett knew.

I'd uncles down that way in the war years,
a whole raft of Merchant Navy engineers,
northern barbarians on the Barbary Coast
in their white ducks, a far cry from Belfast —
old-movie time of transit visas, bad cheques,
the Dakar fiasco, 'Everyone comes to Rick's';
but the proud Berbers of the west resist
the soul-stealing gaze of the 'western' tourist
to nurse the experience of a thousand years
beneath a crescent moon and evening stars
— al-'Dhara, al-'Debaran, al-Qa'id and al-Ta'ir —
peach-pink Arabian nights, the call to prayer
on Lavery's dunes and balconies, austere
as antelope or ibex, a light as rare:
you with your Nikon would go crazy there.

A real barbarian, Wyndham Lewis, in flight
from daily mail, tube station and wireless set,
found there the desert 'blue' tribes he liked best
in the days of the Rif rifles and *Beau Geste,*
far from fake sheikhery and the coast hotels
exploring qasba art in the lunar hills —
'the best this side of China, I should say'.
Of course, most things are different since his day:
looking like Katie Tyrrell and the old folks
in your own 'sublimely gloomy' Athy pix,
as everywhere the filmable populations
have now been framed in shinier compositions,
the open prison of the corporate whole,
for even dissent has long been marketable —
even in the desert of legend and dark myth,
of drought and genocide, what Patti Smith
calls 'the real earth of Rimbaud', few daisies there.
Burroughs and Ginsberg — 9, rue Gît-le-Coeur —
who thought to undermine the monolith
were building new sandcastles in the air.

Back now on the *rive gauche* and the Pont des Arts
re-reading the works of Bonnefoy and Éluard,
a *flâneur* in the dense galaxies of text
yet somehow knowing what to look for next,
I resist Miller's *Quiet Days in Clichy*
to browse among the picture books, *cliché*
and time exposure, the once bright machines,
the mirrored nudes like open nectarines,
high-definition fashion, *Paris de Nuit,*
copperplate silence, cranes at Saint-Denis,
the soap and tickets, the oblivious snow,
a gargoyle musing on the lights below,
soft-focus studio filter work, the glow
and heartening realism of Robert Doisneau
(industrial suburbs, the great aerial one
of the Renault plant beside the Bois de Boulogne,

pensioners, tramps, young lovers in a park,
a kiss at rush hour or a dance in the dark);
and on the history shelves the wartime books,
old coats and bicycles, old hats and specs,
old sniper rifles, Gloria and Étoile
ripping up tarmac in the place Saint-Michel;
at the Gare du Nord a 24-hour clock,
clanking transports, faces wreathed in smoke
and the damned logo everywhere you look;
midnight editions, by Gironde or Loire
a distant grumble in the sky somewhere,
a shaky flashlight piercing night and cloud,
low voices murmuring like owls in a wood.
— Days of resistance, *un peu soviétique,*
plain Sartre and Beauvoir dancing cheek to cheek!

    Now our resistance is to co-optation,
the 'global' project of world domination,
the generative darkness hid from sight
in an earth strung with deterministic light
no more than a ganglion of wires and flex,
crap advertising and commercial sex.
Still sceptical, statistically off-line France
resists the specious arguments most advance,
the digital movies and unnatural nosh,
to stick with real tomatoes, real *brioche*
and real stars like Adjani and Binoche.

    'No art without the resistance of the medium':
our own resistance to the murderous tedium
of business culture lays claim to the real
not as a product but as its own ideal —
live seizures in the flux, fortuitous archetypes,
an art as fugitive as the life it snaps
tracing the magic of some primitive place
in the last retrenchment of the human face,
gossip and pigeons, close-ups by Kertész,

the young Diana in her London crèche.
Us snappers-up of photogenic details,
yourself a snapper of immortal souls,
resist commodity, the *ersatz*, the cold,
the *Schrecklichkeit* of the post-modern world,
that the sun-writing of our resistance days
shine like Cape Clear glimpsed in a heat haze.

    After so much neglect, resolved anew,
creative anarchy I come back to you,
not the faux anarchy of media culture
but the real chaos of indifferent nature —
for instance, my own New Year resolution
is to study weather, clouds and their formation,
going straight to video with each new release
untroubled by the ignorant thought police.
I wish you good light or a light in a mist
safe from the critic and the invasive tourist,
a Munster twilight far from the venal roar
where waifs and strays can beat paths to your door,
unseasonal creatures, ears against the sky,
and timorous things that wouldn't hurt a fly,
conceptual silence, the best place to live —
'*Que faire d'une lampe, il pleut, le jour se lève*':
real daylight keeps on breaking, in other words.
So, love to Hammond and the karate kids.
Down silent paths, in secret hiding places,
the locked out-house that no one notices,
listening for footfalls by a quiet river
the sun will find us when the worst is over,
when everyone is in love, our children laugh
at the gruff bloke snuffling in the epigraph
and in the window frame a persistent fly
buzzes with furious life which will never die.

Lapis Lazuli

(for Harry Clifton)

A whole night sky that serves as a paperweight,
this azure block blown in from the universe
sits on my desk here, a still shimmering piece
of planet rock speckled with gold and white,
coarse-grained and knobbly as a meteorite
though recognized as a 'gem' in its own right.
The willow-pattern wisdom is still unknown,
the twinkling sages and the branchy house;
for this is the real thing in its natural state,
the raw material from which art is born.

Growth night-formed in sun-struck Afghanistan,
this complex chunk of sulphurous silicates
— a royal blue loved since the earth began
because, like the swirling sea, it never dates —
blinks authenticity through mysterious days
of slowly moving cloud and watery haze,
days of silence, watching as paint dries
while Buddha and a Yeats head supervise.
Dim in the half-light of conventional rain,
we start at the squeal of Berkeley's telephone.

Slow fires still glowing in our cindery grates
even while the white, meridional sun vibrates
on sandy shelves where life first crept ashore,
we need the glitter of those secret depths
like the loved women of our private myths.
On dark dawns that look for that subtle gleam
and blinking noons obtuse to its dark dream
when slow thought replaces the money-shower,
we want the key to that impervious heart:
with ultramarine what need have we of art?

Heat lightning photographs the astonished sea.
Am I in Bermuda or in cold Sakhalin? Either
this new century with its bewildering weather
will work wonders for the sea-angling industry
or bring wolves dancing down the mooring ropes
of vast tankers and patronizing warships
to spill the bins and skate on the ice floes.
Do we die laughing or are we among those
for whom a spectre, some discredited ghost
still haunts the misty windows of old hopes?

While planes that consume deserts of gasoline
darken the sun in another rapacious war
a young woman reads alone in a lighted train,
scratches her scalp and shoves specs in her hair,
skipping the obvious for the rich and rare.
Hope lies with her as it always does really
and the twinkling sages in the Deux Magots
first glimpsed by a student forty years ago
on a continent like a plain of lapis lazuli;
and the Eurostar glides into the Gare du Nord.

Heathrow

Drugs, razors, cameras; *Lucozade replaces
lost energy*, even in the strangest cases.

Hampstead Graves

The last resting-places at peace in mid-July —
white click of cricket from a previous age
beyond the headstones and the boundary hedge.
Did Keats or Coleridge ever get down here?
Not open yet, and too far from the Heath.
Above the angels the planes shine and fly,
angels and insects; above willow, birch,
the modest outline of a local church,
some inscriptions buried by flower and leaf:
Mary-Anne, Miriam, Arthur, Jamal, Elizabeth
for ever in our hearts, who quit this life
... devoted father; dearly belovèd wife ...
the Celtic love-knot, the six-pointed star,
the Islamic sickle, simple as a scimitar;
and the rear windows, blue suburban skies,
deckchair and brick, the penetrable mysteries.

'Things'

(for Jane)

It rained for years when I was young.
I sat there as in the old pop song
and stared at a lonely avenue
like everybody else I knew
until, one day, the sun came out.
I too came out, to shout and sing
and see what it was all about.
Oh yes, I remember everything.

The Cloud Ceiling

(for Maisie)

An ocean-drop, dash in the dark, flash in the brain,
suspension in the red mist, in the light-grain,
a twitching silence in the hiding place,
fine pearly night-glow of the forming face,
the pushing brow, the twirling ears and knees . . .
Space girl, soap on a rope, you like cloud-swing,
bath water and world music; a kidney-bean,
you lie there dreaming on your knotted string
listening hard with shut, determined eyes —
a soul of barely determinate shape and size.

Are thoughts a tap trickle, a cloud formation?
Given to light readings and rich inactivity,
alternative galaxies, atonal composition
and tentative revisions of quantum gravity,
you float in a universe of unspoken words
far from the bright lights and story-boards.
A shy girl in your own private microcosm,
you travel from cloud-chasm to cloud-chasm
awaiting the moment when the burbles start,
the camera action, the first signs of art;

and enter like one of Aristophanes' cloud chorus
heard 'singing in the distance' though not for us,
daughters of ocean for whom alone we write,
grave sisters of the rainbow, rose and iris
who dip their pitchers in the sea at night
and soak the risen leaf before first light —
capricious dirigibles of the swirling ether,
great wringing sacks above the luminous earth
from whose precipitations images gather
as in the opacity of a developing-bath.

You open your eyes, the blue of children's eyes.
Sunlight streams like April at the window

and sky flocks graze above your dreaming head,
spinning deliriously round your baby bed.
We've painted a cloud ceiling, a splash of stars
in the attic studio where you lie safe
like yin and yang in your own secret life.
The indeterminate firmament is yours.
Life is a dream of course, as we all know,
but one to be dreamt in earnest even so.

I who, though soft-hearted, always admired
granite and blackthorn and the verse hard-wired,
tingle and flow like January thaw water
in contemplation of this rosy daughter.
Be patient with an old bloke; remember later
one who, in his own strange, distracted youth
awake to the cold stars for the harsh truth,
now tilts a bottle to your open mouth.
So drench the nappies; fluff, bubble and burp:
I probably won't be here when you've grown up.

During the War

(for Hugh Haughton)

There are those of us who say 'during the war'
as if the insane scramble for global power
doesn't continue much as it did before.
Red buses and black taxis then as now
in thundering London, even in sloppy Soho.
The light-bowl flickers and the lifts are slow
but I bounce on sneakers up a winding stair:
even at sixty I can still walk on air.

I'm reading Bowen again in mysterious Kôr
and picturing the black-out in Regent's Park,
fierce moonlight blazing down on rail and door,
lost lovers, changing lights, fugitive smiles,
one car, silence, ponds white in the dark,
the whole place clearly visible for miles —
now visible, a bright smudge, from outer space.
No serious myth since the first days of 'peace'.

This morning in Wardour St., a skip, a tip,
a broken pipe, some unfinished repair work.
A basin of mud and junk has choked it up,
reflecting the blown sky and a baroque
cloud cinema beyond earthly intercourse:
a hole in the road where cloud leaves gather,
each one framed for a moment in stagnant water
and trailing out of the picture in due course.

This is nothing, this is the triumph of time,
waste products mixing in the history bin,
rain ringing with a harsh, deliberate chime
on scrap iron, plastic and depleted tin,
its grim persistence under the rush-hour sky
a nuisance to the retail trade. Andrei
on his back, wounded, during his own war:
'I never really saw the sky before ...'

They're filming a mini-series down below.
Strip lighting writes the dusk out everywhere
on corporate space and stadium, while slow
flashes go racing up like tracer fire
and lasers fence among the clouds for show.
The spiteful rain, filmic, begins to freeze,
grown sentimental and considering snow;
flies as it lies, reluctant to lie low.

December night; night vision; a slash of hail.
An east wind gathering force on water streams
up here like shirts blown from the shining Thames
to Ronnie Scott's and Mme. JoJo's, Soho Jazz & Soul.
Time now to watch for the dawn of a new age.
Down there, gleaming amid the porn and veg,
its rippling skin mutating by the minute,
a shivering dump with one faint star in it.

Jean Rhys in Kettner's

I

I'm crouching here in the corner, a kind of ghost
but safe with my Craven 'A' and Gordon's gin,
wearing a cloche hat and an old fox fur
and skimming *Vogue* with my distracted air.
The rush-hour crowd a hail storm ushers in
heaves at the bar like flotsam in flat seas
(I looked it up: *sargaço*, n., Portuguese)
and scares me slightly in the window seat
where I shiver, no doubt looking a bit lost
remembering cane fields in Dominican heat,
a gone-with-the-windward isle of the unblest,
the harsh plantations and the dark voyage
— somewhere I lived once in another age
with thunder, magic and the scent of jasmine.

2

Not easy being a woman in the old world —
the quick presumption, the frank stare as though
one achieved little on this earth, at least
little of what the wise world calls achieving.
Reader, I was a tedious, nightmare guest
who never learned the common art of living
but died triumphant and amazed at how
the secrecies I harboured as a child,
under the skin, were recognized at last.
'Writing I don't know; other things I know':
what children now in the gardens of Roseau?
Blown there by the discredited trade winds,
bewitched, bewildered, in at least two minds,
we found no true home in our chosen west.

3

The pianist plays show numbers and thirties jazz.
A slave in my turn, one to be bought and sold,
once hot and anxious, then aghast and cold,
I'd come here with the other chorus girls,
each in a short skirt and a string of pearls,
and men whose eyes were an anonymous glaze.
A life of boarding houses and cheap hotels
and I snag like a torn bag in a thorn-field
snapping and scratching, fighting to keep sane
in a new age; and so the soul survives.
Released at last, I lived out my two lives
between the water and the *vie en rose*:
the bottles ting-a-ling between hedgerows,
a draughty house at the end of a country lane.

The Widow of Kinsale

Cionn tSáile, 'Head of the Tide',
knew me once as a young bride
but those days are gone;
a rock exposed to the sun,
sardonic, cold and stiff,
I go with the ebb of life.

The salt surge in my veins
whispers its age and drains
down to the shrinking sea:
no more high tide for me.
Stylish I was and not
got up in this old coat.

Young ones now think only
of fashion and easy money —
as we did once, except
we never had much of it:
real people were the thing,
to hear them talk and sing.

When I was a girl we thought
more highly of our admirers.
I opened my young body
gravely to their desires;
now I am an old lady,
unwanted and unsought.

War widow and sea widow
many years on the shelf,
I've better things to do
than my once sexy self,
my beauty and high tone
nothing but skin and bone.

I was a fierce temptation
to wild, generous men

of my own generation;
lovingly I would watch
while driving them insane.
Now look at this eyepatch.

Once a wife and mother
beset by childish squabbles,
I live alone with a plethora
of stuff in the loud fridge:
plaice, chops and vegetables,
enough for a new ice age.

I who was bright and gay
in the wine-and-roses years
am briskly polite today
to gossipy old neighbours;
my white head in the clouds,
I avoid the holiday crowds.

Crows croak from the convent
where once we used to skip.
Everything has been taken
since it is not convenient;
the upper windows are broken,
the lower ones boarded up.

Sometimes I drive over
in my olive vintage Rover
to Bantry or even Dingle
and think of the times I knew
when everyone was single;
but now they are so few

that mostly I prefer
a comfortable armchair.
I could re-read for ever
the novels of William Trevor,

that lovely man, and watch
starlight in the dark porch.

Calm and alone at last,
I wake up in the night.
A superstitious atheist,
I now befriend the clergy
and go to church despite
the new revised liturgy;

but my true guiding spirit
is something I inherit,
a thing dim and opaque,
a lighthouse in the fog,
a lamp hung in a wood
to light my solitude,

breastplate and consolation
whatever the situation:
increasing aches and pains,
the silence in the womb
as the life force wanes,
my children far from home.

Peewits run on the strand
as evening light warms
primitive life forms,
islands of shining sand,
and the ebb tide withdraws
with a chuckle of bony claws.

A Garden God

A bomber fly flits from the ruined mouth;
from the eye socket an inquisitive moth.

Bashō in Kinsale

Samurai cries from
Enthusiasts in the gym
As I wander home.

Dithery rain lines;
Crows glisten in the branches
Of listening pines.

Gulls in the clear air,
Hawthorn snow in the hedges;
Soon you will be here.

March, evening shadow
On pine and quiet dockyard
Here in Hokkaido.

Clouds obscure the night
Giving our eyes a rest from
The intense moonlight.

Rough sea after dark;
Blazing over the harbour
The fierce zodiac.

A heron voice harsh
Above us after midnight
Like a lightning flash.

Walking each evening
At a slower pace, we hear
The dark river sing.

A morning of mist;
No light source but a hidden
Sun burns in the east.

A cove, flies and fleas,
Wrack magic in salt sea air
And the faintest breeze.

The seal surfaces.
Around her in the water
A cloud disperses.

These old childish things,
Big blisters at the shoreline,
Are my water wings.

Blown sand and no talk,
Even the most northern road
An easier walk.

Watching us, the earth
Has all the time in the world
For death and rebirth.

Desert island books:
Homer and Rachel Carson,
Durable hardbacks.

Sketch of a sail race,
The work of many summers:
A few lines in space.

Sand Studies

Driftwood and cloud castle,
expiring lines of froth,
absorbing sand where every
worm-hole is a discovery:
two worlds, earth and air;
water, the best of both.

Breakwater, an ebbing tide,
the frantic shingle dash
and vigilant gull glide,
cold eyes on whatever blind
nourishment the wave-wash,
receding, leaves behind.

These photographs, these
vitreous transparencies
expose each bare feature:
original rock sculpture,
rubble and ropes of cream
as graphic as any dream.

This one, taken at night
or nearly, shows a flight
of clustering sun splinters,
a rippling archipelago
of silvery star cinders
the light left long ago.

There is a special calm
in the rising sea level;
quietude, cool but warm,
the surface a hushed veil
where you expect a fin
or a spinning dolphin.

Closer in, slipping aside
from the furious tide race,

a swirl of incoming tide
has signed a separate peace
with sighs and whisperings,
its ripples silent strings,

each one a thoughtful stave
next to the bath-house roar,
air garden and wind bower
where each slow-motion wave
is a blue note designed
to calm the riotous mind —

proposing, like a soul breeze
or random natural noise,
a new kind of 'found'
spirit-breathing music:
not pop, please, but the basic
tones of an ancient sound.

Resistant, a losing struggle,
the breakwater descends
from quick-shelving sands;
seaward the stanchions stride
into the roar and giggle
of a punctual high tide.

The long contingent action
of salt on the first rocks,
a never ceasing friction,
no respite and no pity:
this is the raw reality,
always that harsh index.

You want a serene old age?
Cold front and icy ridge,
briny bubble and squeak
and the tributary leak

are waiting for you here;
flea wrack, a stench of tar —

and the ancient art of leisure
best practised not on any
petrol-blue *côte d'azur*
with its bums and money
but in the fresh exposure
of a single sea anemone.

Wrack whips whistle and snore,
then near-silence once more
as the tide reconsiders;
rough face of the waters.
But flick of a wren-wing
and she sits on a rock to sing.

Where to Hide

(Some derelict beach hut or abandoned wreck
as in that strange novel by Yann Queffélec.)

New Wave

On the first day of principal photography
they sit outside at a Saint-Germain café
with coffee cups between them on a round
table of chequered oilcloth red and grey.
The hand-held camera looks for natural light,
mikes pick up traffic and incidental sound.
A mid-week noon and the hot bridges sweat;
from ice buckets, from windows, watches, knives,
life flashes back at them their glittering lives.

Silence, the first thing they have in common,
creates a little precise hole in the uproar
and the vague sorrow between man and woman
changes summer to autumn as they conspire
like scientists working from the same data.
When they reach Cabourg beyond a darkening road
and a white hotel room shaken by white waves
in a cloud of powder and brine, they run baths
and stare at the moon through open windows.

While the lamps go off along the promenade
they wake to a dawn silence, curtained light,
mist and roar of the sea, vast dazzling cloud;
but the stripped mind, still moist and nocturnal,
flinches from confrontation with the infinite.
The sky, its racing stripes and ice-cream colours,
thin cries of children from the beach below,
and the hurtling gulls, are too heartbreaking;
they shut the shutters and return to the dark.

They live the hours as others live the years.
A plane sky-writes, sails flock on the horizon,
their sheets stretch to the white lines of surf
and they doze as if on their own patch of sand
with wind and sun combing their backs and thighs
in a dream of dune-light and rustling quartz
worn smooth by night winds since the dawn of time.

Air reigns, mother-of-pearl; flies come and go;
they open and close their fists like the newly born.

He has given up even on the death of language
and a shower of dots relieves his final page ...
A singer, tonight she sings in the casino
to a shiny ring of bourgeois, but her heart
has already taken flight from the car park.
Tide-click; starry wavelengths; aquarium light
from the old world picks out in a double row
their sandy prints where, orphans going home,
they climb back into the waves in a snow of foam.

Circe and Sirens

Homer was right to break the story up —
flash back, fast forward to another beach,
another island. As the sun rose and shone
they headed inland and found Circe's place
in its dim glade, a pavilion of white stone,
a ribbon of woodsmoke rising from the thatch
where wolves and lions, dozy from sedatives,
lived out their nodding, soporific lives;
the men, recovered from her magic cup,
relaxed and sprawled at ease about the house.

He took the prophylactic. 'Sail,' she said,
'over the water to the Cimmerian coast,
those dark people shrouded in fog and mist.
Beside a grim, fast-flowing river bed
there is a grove where rustling willows grow;
dig a trench there out of the leafy mud
and you will see a multitude of the dead,
their curious shadows whispering to and fro,
come up to look at you. Amid that host
speak to your mother and Tiresias' ghost.'

Among the wives and daughters of the great
— Jocasta, Ariadne, Phaedra — he came upon
his mother Anticleia who whispered, 'Son,
this is no place for you, why are you here
with these lost spirits? What capricious fate
brings you among us before your time is due?'
Tiresias appeared. 'You will be late
in getting home,' said he, 'in a bad state,
with a strange ship, all your companions gone;
yet you will die contented and ashore.'

And there he recognized young Elpenor,
a foolish drunken fellow who'd slept off
a party on the tiles and with the dawn,
woken up by the others' rush and din,

stumbled and fell headlong from Circe's roof.
'Remember me,' he cried. 'Burn my remains,
bury my ashes on the grey seashore
and for a gravestone plant the shapely oar
I pulled when I was alive among my friends.'
The thing was done and they set off once more.

The Sirens sang: 'Odysseus, slow down! —
Sailors who hear us from their painted ships
never forget the sweet sound of our voices,
the enchanted music issuing from our lips';
but, agitated and wild-eyed, he sailed on
to thundering cave and overhanging cliff,
loud breakers, wandering rocks and sucking surf.
Sheet lightning tore the timbers from their places
and corpses bobbed like seagulls on the sea;
but, clinging to a spar, he floated free.

'. . . if you survive,' Tiresias warned, 'the few
remaining dangers you have yet to face
and the temptations being prepared for you.'
Dangers he had expected, not another
island, its dune songs and erotic weather
where he might stop indefinitely moreover
and his restorative visit last for years.
He might retire, sea music in his ears,
this micro-climate his last resting place,
and spend his old age in sublime disgrace.

Calypso

Homer was wrong, she never 'ceased to please'.
Once he'd escaped from Circe's magic castle,
the toxic cup, shape-shifting witcheries;
from the underworld, from Aeolus' watery roar,
the high-pitched Sirens' penetrating whistle,
cliff monsters, divine anger, broken boats,
on soft, tinkling shingle he crept ashore
through juniper and parsley, cows and goats,
and found the hot path to her open door,
a cart parked in the lane, a smoking fire.

Gaily distracting him from his chief design
she welcomed him with open arms and thighs,
teaching alternatives to war and power.
A wild girl rushing to the head like wine,
she held him closely with her braided coils,
her swift insistence, aromatic oils,
her mild, beguiling glance, tuning his days
to a slow sea rhythm; and through a salty haze
he watched her moving as in a golden shower
or swimming with her nymphs from the seashore.

Red sails in the sunset where the dripping prows
rapped out a drum rhythm on uncertain seas
of skimming birds, a lonely pine or shrine —
but the sea's secrets diminished on dry land,
darker than they could know or understand,
and vanished in a blink, night coming on
wherever they put ashore to rest. A whorled
conch whispered about a recent, far-off world
with oars sunk in sand marking the graves
of those lost to chance or vindictive waves.

Some harsh, some murderous with savage gulls
squatting in triumph amid scattered skulls
buzzing with flies, he knew unfortunate isles,
the eternal conflict between sea and stone,

the palpitating heat of the noon sun.
He prayed for an end to these moronic wars,
burned wasteful sacrifices to the vague stars
and dreamed of honey, yoghurt, figs and wine
on night beaches far from the life he knew,
silent, unlit; but a faint murmur, a faint glow.

Those were the times he thought about his wife,
remembering their lives in a former life,
her handsome profile, her adventurous heart
and proud demeanour. At sea and lost he wept
for jokes and music, promises unkept,
sandals on board and tile, shared places, friends,
shared history, origins, those woods and glens,
his brisk departure from the family hearth
a glib mistake; but nature took its course
leaving him desolation and long remorse.

Ithaca, 'home', not far now as the kite flew,
he sniffed those evenings when a sea wind blew
but lingered in that cave house behind the dunes
enchanted now by hazel and sea-grey eyes,
the star-flow of the hair, the skittish tones,
sand-quivering foam, long leisure, lip and gland
in the early-morning light, the sun ablaze
through leaves and linen, through her open hand,
briar and cumuli; so the years unwound
to a whisper of spring water and kitchen noise.

Homer was right though about the important thing,
the redemptive power of women; for this narrative,
unlike the blinding shields, is womanly stuff.
The witch bewitches, the owl-winged sisters sing,
some kind girl takes charge within the shadow
of a calm glade where the sea finds a meadow;
much-sought Penelope in her new resolute life
has wasted no time acting the stricken widow

and even the face that sank the final skiff
knows more than beauty; beauty is not enough.

Penelope, of course, with the husband gone,
was instantly besieged by plausible men
and the wild rumours now in circulation;
the palace, ruined by competing suitors,
hosted intrigue, conspiracy and confusion,
its shadow crumbling in Ionian waters.
He knew nothing of this; or, if he did,
felt he had no more heart now for a fight,
asking the Pleiades or a drifting cloud
to let these things unravel as best they might.

He spent his days there in a perpetual summer.
Stuck in a rock-cleft like a beachcomber
washed up, high and dry amid luminous spray,
intent on pond life, wildflowers and wind play,
the immense significance of a skittering ant,
a dolphin-leap or a plunging cormorant,
he learned to live at peace with violent nature,
calm under the skies' grumbling cloud-furniture
and bored by practical tackle, iron and grease —
an ex-king and the first philosopher in Greece.

Bemused with his straw hat and driftwood stick,
unmoved by the new wars and the new ships,
he died there, fame and vigour in eclipse,
listening to voices echo, decks and crates
creak in the harbour like tectonic plates —
or was he sharp still in his blithe disgrace,
deliberate pilot of his own foggy shipwreck?
Homer was wrong, he never made it back; or,
if he did, spent many a curious night hour
still questioning that strange, oracular face.

Harbour Lights

And I . . . a mere newcomer whose ancestors had inhabited the earth so briefly that my presence was almost anachronistic.
— Rachel Carson, *The Edge of the Sea*

It's one more sedative evening in Co. Cork.
The house is quiet and the world is dark
while the Bush gang are doing it to Iraq.
The flesh is weary and I've read the books;
nothing but lies and nonsense on the box
whose light-dot vanishes with a short whine
leaving only a grey ghost in the machine.
Slick boats click at the quayside down below
the drowsy bungalows of the well-to-do;
late light illuminates the closing pub,
shop window, leisure centre and sailing club,
exhausted cars tucked up in their garages,
rabbits and foxes, birds dumb in the hedges;
midsummer light shifting its general blaze
sets in a secret thicket of hazel trees,
on garden sheds and lined pre-Cambrian rock
red as the wavy roof tiles of Languedoc.
Re-reading history page by lamplit page,
imagining the lost poems of Iníon Dubh,
I could be living here in another age
except at weekends when the bikes converge.
Blow-in asylum and dormitory of privilege,
its dreamy woods are straight out of Chekhov,
quaint gardens made for 19th-century love;
transnational, the skies are Indian skies,
the harbour lights Chinese or Japanese;
and certain thatchy corners the gull sees
keep the last traces of the bardic phase,
straw spaces echoing to disconsolate cries.

Get out more? I prefer to watch by starlight
the London plane, a galaxy in flight,
night-shining cloud, a ghost ship among stars,

and the light fading from our western shores.
It's now that the high spirits begin to drop,
remembering buried errors and wasted time;
but in the morning when the sun comes up
there will be snail mail with its pearly gleam
and a gruff husky scratching on the gravel,
young people chattering as in a Russian novel,
sky-shining roofs where smoky notions rise,
back yards where the drainpipes soliloquize,
a wood-shriek as a whining saw spins free
and the wild soul flies from a stricken tree.
Alive to voices and, to my own surprise,
up with the lark, up with the June sunrise,
I study the visible lines of tidal flow,
the spidery leaves alight with sweat and dew,
doors blazing primary colours, blue and red,
phone-lines at angles against piling cloud.

Go wandering with your stick on the back road,
you start with a ruined convent school, a tough
chough cursing you from a lichen-speckled roof;
organic fields to the left; and, to the right,
the mud basin of one more building site.
Startling how fast a thing can integrate:
beneath those tiles some immigrant teenager
will write the secret poetry of the future.
Sun-ripples on the trout-shimmering Bandon River
where on a clear day you can see for ever;
a flash of foam like Gray's *Great Wave at Sète*,
alternate light and shade on the shut eyes,
the untaken photograph and the unwritten phrase;
woof of a terrier, crash of a fluttering wing,
the bird-voiced tinkle of a hidden spring.
Now, note that white sail where a dinghy moves,
a raw strand where Cúchulainn fought the waves,
a writhing Daphne hawthorn, hands and hair
mute but articulate in the Atlantic air,

chained in the ivy strings that bind her there
while somebody takes shape in the heat haze:
a young woman in tracksuit and running shoes.
A cloud covers the sun and a quick shower
scribbles with many pencils on the estuary,
the coves, the beaches and the open sea,
sub-tropical wave-light where it calmly roars
at dark soul-cottages with their shining doors,
the docks in fierce, eye-straining definition,
each thing distinct but in oblique relation;
the faux schooner bearing a famous name,
a pocket cruise ship like a video game.

   Back at the house revisit the dark grove
of baths, old cars and fridges, while above
a withered orchard the slow cloud-cranes move
in the empty silence where a myth might start
— flute-note, god-word — the first whisper of art
withdrawn in its integrity, in its own
obscurity, for not everything need be known.
Magic survives only where blind profit,
so quick on the uptake, takes no notice of it
for ours is a crude culture dazed with money,
a flighty future that would ditch its granny.
The orchard withers but the birds sing on
through the long morning, and in the afternoon
you watch clouds gather and disperse, paint dry,
and listen patiently to the wasp and fly.

   But everything is noticed, everything known
in the 'knowledge era', advertised as the one
without precedent; though in late middle age,
striving to tame the Yeatsian lust and rage,
I claim the now disgraceful privilege
of living part-time in a subversive past:
'... fall and are built again'; nor is this the last,
for the tough nuts, imagining you fortunate,

will aim to get you with their curious hate.
Try the Blue Haven, its interior bright
with port-holes and chronometers, spare parts;
winking in turn, a frieze of lighthouse charts.

Lady, whose shrine stands on the promontory
above the fancy golf course, taking inventory
of vapour trails and nuclear submarines,
keep close watch on our flight paths and sea lanes,
our tourist coaches and our slot machines,
the cash dynamic and the natural gas.
Your arbour stands there as it always has,
secret and shy above these baffling shores
and the white-winged oceanic water table.
A short path and a tumbler of fresh flowers,
a cup of dusty water, bead and pebble,
the salt-whipped plaster of your serious head,
an azure radiance in your tiny shed
gazing out over the transatlantic cable
with a chipped eye towards Galicia and the Azores.

I toy with cloud thoughts as an alternative
to the global shit storm that we know and love,
but unsustainable levels of aviation
have complicated this vague resolution;
for even clouds are gobbled up by the sun,
not even the ethereal clouds are quite immune:
these too will be marketed if it can be done.
I was here once before, though, at Kinsale
with the mad chiefs, and lived to tell the tale;
I too froze in the hills, first of the name
in Monaghan, great my pride and great my shame —
or was it a slander that we tipped them off,
old Hugh asking a quart of Power's from Taaffe?
Does it matter now? Oh yes, it still matters;
strange currents circulate in these calm waters
though we don't mention them, we talk instead

of the new golf course out at the Old Head.
What have I achieved? Oh, little enough, God knows:
some dubious verse and some ephemeral prose;
as for the re-enchantment of the sky,
that option was never really going to fly
but it's too late to do much about it now
except to trust in the contumacious few
who aren't afraid to point to an obvious truth,
and the frank stare of unpredictable youth.

    A buoy nods faintly in the harbour mouth
as I slope down to the front for a last walk
and watch trawlers disgorging at the dock
in the loud work-glow of a Polish freighter,
dark oil drums and fish boxes on the quay,
winches and ropes, intestines of the sea
alive with the stench of pre-historic water.
I've noted codgers, when the day is done,
sitting in easy rows in the evening sun
before the plate-faced rising moon creates
a sphere of influence where thought incubates
with midnight oil and those old harbour lights,
'the harbour lights that once brought you to me'.
White page, dark world; wave theory; moon and pines:
thin as an aspirin that vast surface shines,
the pits and heights in intimate close-up,
her bowed head grave as through a telescope
as if aware of danger; for quite soon,
perhaps, we dump our rubbish on the moon.
The new dark ages have been fiercely lit
to banish shadow and the difficult spirit;
yet here, an hour from the night-shining city
ablaze with its own structural electricity,
sporadic pinpoints star the archaic night
older and clearer than any glow we generate.

Outside the exhausted kids have wandered home;
the house is quiet, calm till the next storm:
when the time comes and if the coast is clear,
work in some sort of order, let me hear
the cries of children playing but not too near.
Tick of real time, the dark realities
in the unreality of the mental gaze;
a watery murmur, a drip of diesel oil,
night silence listening to the dozy soul,
the waves' confusion in the void. 'No dice',
said Einstein; but each bit of rock might claim
a different origin if it took its time,
the slightest life with its amoebic wobble
might tell us otherwise if it took the trouble
and even the tiniest night-rustling pebble
might solve the mystery if it had a voice;
for everything is water, the world a wave,
whole populations quietly on the move.

Will the long voyage end here among friends
and swimming with a loved one from white strands,
the sea loud in our veins? It never ends
or ends before we know it, for everyone
'stands at the heart of life, pierced by the sun,
and suddenly it's evening' (Quasimodo);
suddenly we're throwing a longer shadow.
The hermit crab crawls to its holiday home;
dim souls wriggle in seething chaos, body
language and new thought forming there already
in hidden depths and exposed rock oases,
those secret cultures where the sky pauses,
sand flats, a whispery fringe discharging gases,
a white dish drained by the receding sea
and trailing runic whips of tangled hair
brushed and combed by the tide, exhaling air.
No, this is Galápagos and the old life-force
rides Daz and Exxon to the blinding surface.

Down there a drenching of the wilful sperm,
congenital sea fight of the shrimp and worm
with somewhere the soft impulse of a lover,
the millions swarming into pond and river
to find the right place, find it and live for ever.

Biographia Literaria

A spoilt child shivers at the river's edge —
night-hiding yes but anxious to be found,
a troubled soul torn between fear and rage.
Sun, moon and star on the sky-blue clock face
in the south transept of St Mary's mind
the autumn dark, and shadows have changed place
obscurely, each tick an 'articulate sound',
as he dozes off under a rustic bridge.

When he wakes at dawn to a slow-waning moon,
frozen and scared, curled up like the unborn,
the sun blinking behind an owl-eyed barn,
frost in the fields and winter coming on,
a frigate flutters on a glittering sea.
A great cold has gripped the heart already
with signs of witchery in an ivy tree:
now nothing will ever be the same again.

Genie, taper and paper, long solitary cliff walks,
cloud thoughts unfolding over the Quantocks
sheer to shore beneath high, feathery springs.
The cottage shines its light above the rocks,
the world's oceans tear in from the west
and an Aeolian harp the size of a snuff-box
sings in a casement where its tingling strings
record the faintest whisper, the loudest blast.

Receptive, tense, adrift in a breezy trance,
the frame is seized as if in a nightmare
by some quotation, fugue, some fugitive air,
some distant echo of the primal scream.
Silence, dead calm, no worldly circumstance;
the words form figures and begin to dance —
and then the miracle, the pleasure dome,
the caves of ice, the vibrant dulcimer.

Stowey to Göttingen, philosophy in a mist,
wide-eyed sublimities of ghost and *Geist*,
wild wind-and-rain effects of Greta Hall,
the rattling windows and the icy lake,
babbling excursions and the perpetual
white roaring rose of a close waterfall;
finally Highgate Grove and table talk,
a 'destined harbour' for the afflicted soul.

Asra and Christabel in confused opium dreams,
heartbroken whimpers and nocturnal screams
grow ever fainter as he becomes 'a sage
escaped from the inanity', aghast
at furious London and its rising smoke,
the sinister finance of a dark new age.
Dunn's pharmacy is only a short walk;
his grown-up daughter visits him there at last.

Trigorin

(Chekhov, *The Seagull,* Act 4)

The towns where the train pauses manufacture
chimneys and fences, boredom, mud and birches.
A cool breeze flaps decrepit architecture
and blows a white blaze on the country roads,
vegetable gardens, grimy local churches.
Dead souls are sleeping in the autumn woods;
at Tver', only a hundred versts from Moscow,
a wandering gull foreshadows the first snow.

The clouds are grand pianos; he makes a note.
Gogolian porters blink in smoky shadows,
a scent of heliotrope and a buzz of flies.
Girl in a blouse, man in a linen suit;
the wind goes running in remembered meadows
under the vast light of these northern skies:
'Out here I feel a quickening of the senses
far from reviewers and hostile audiences.'

Nina, he's come this time for a last look
at the great forest and your native lake,
the clear freshwater ripples you deserted
to join the theatre for his sake and yours.
He let you down of course, and himself too:
his work fell off when he lost sight of you.
Your soul migrated from his icy art;
a stuffed gull listens from a chest of drawers.

Watch out, he's working on a new novel,
his best yet; when it sees the light of day
critics, as usual, will find it slight,
adroitly done though not a patch on Tolstoy.
(So too the friends gathered around his grave:
'Oh, a great gift, if not quite Turgenev . . .')
A dead seagull, what a terrific story;
amazing if you too were there tonight —

and there you are now, tapping the windowpane
like a tense revenant or a familiar ghost.
Waves on the water, wind loud in the wood
with a raw October evening drawing in,
but nobody loves each other as they should.
All come and go, to the hotel, the train,
the gun room and the verandah; all begin
to die, it will be twenty years at most.

Brian Moore's Belfast

(*for Gerald Dawe*)

The last trams were still running in those days.
People wore hats and gloves as long before;
raw fissures lingered where incendiaries
demolished Clifton St. in April of '41:
the big band era, dances and commotion,
but the war ended and rain swept once more
parks and playgrounds, chapel and horse trough
'to die in the faraway mists over Belfast Lough'.

Do this, do that, road closed, no entry, stop! —
a world of signs and yet the real thing too:
even now I catch a whiff of brack and bap,
the soap and ciggies of the *disparus*.
Buns from Stewart's, gobstoppers from Graham's,
our crowd intent on our traditional games,
sectarian puzzlement, a swinging rope,
freezing winters, pristine bicycle frames;

school windows under the Cave Hill, childish faces,
uncles and aunties, pipes and lipstick traces,
epiphanies in sheds and woody places:
how can we not love the first life we knew?
'We can dream only what we know,' he said.
I know the whole length of the Antrim Road
and often think of Salisbury Avenue;
mysterious Hazelwood, I still dream of you.

On Riverside Drive and a California dream beach
such things revisited him, just out of reach,
just as he left them after Naples, Warsaw,
frozen for ever in the austere post-war
where frequent silence keeps its own integrity
and smoky ghosts of the exhausted city
rustle with phantom life whose time is up.
They queue in Campbell's crowded coffee shop

or wait for a bus at Robb's. I can make out
a clutch of gantries, a white sepulchre
grimly vigilant on its tiny acre,
skirts and shirts mid-20th-century style
in dimly lit arcades, carpets of wet
grain at the quayside where a night boat
churns up the dark and a rapturous old girl
sings 'Now Is the Hour' with her eternal smile.

Insomnia

Scratch of a match
fierce in the dark. The alarm clock,
night-vigilant, reads twenty minutes to four;
wide awake, as so often at this dead hour,
I gaze down at the lighted dock,
trawler and crated catch,
as if on watch.

The bright insects
of helicopters drop to the decks
of gas rigs ten miles out in the heavy waves,
their roaring rotors far from our quiet leaves,
before midnight, and the ship that shone
at dusk on the horizon
has long since gone.

Nothing stirs
in garden or silent house,
no night owl flies or none that we can hear;
not even the mild, traditional fieldmouse
runs nibbling, as you'd expect, under the stairs.
Boats knock and click at the pier,
shrimps worship the stars.

The whole coast
is soporific as if lost
to echoes of a distant past —
the empty beach house with no obvious owner,
the old hotel like a wrecked ocean liner
washed up one stormy night
and left to rot.

That woman from
the Seaview, a 'blow-in'
of some kind from a foreign shore,
seems out of her element and far from home,
the once perhaps humorous eyes grown vague out here.

What is she? A Lithuanian, or a Finn?
We've met before

beside some flat
road bridge or bleak strand road,
two men in black at the corner staring hard,
far off in the stricken distance perhaps a shipyard,
chimneys, power plants, gasometers,
oil refineries, Gothic spires
and things like that —

where a cloud climbs
and swirls, yellow and red
streaking the estuary, and a soul screams
for sunken origins, for the obscure sea bed
and glowing depths, the alternative mud haven
we left behind. Once more we live in
'interesting times'.

Somewhere the Wave

Once more the window and a furious fly
shifting position, niftier on the pane
than the slow liner or the tiny plane.
Dazzled by the sun, dazed by the rain,
today this frantic speck against the sky,
so desperate to get out in the open air
and cruise among the roses, starts to know
not all transparency is come and go.

But the window opens like an opened door
so the wild fly escapes to the airstream,
the raw crescendo of the crashing shore
and 'a radical astonishment at existence' —
a voice, not quite a voice, in the sea distance
listening to its own thin cetaceous whistle,
sea music gasp and sigh, slow wash and rustle.
Somewhere the wave is forming which in time . . .

Tara Boulevard

Amazed by the shining towers were she alive,
she wouldn't know the downtown skyline now
— Coke, Delta Airlines, CNN, King Drive —
but ten miles south, in many a back yard,
it's going to be another day tomorrow
on an imaginary plantation where
the Ibo sat once to their hominy grits;
in Jonesboro, 'O'Hara Gas' and 'Body Parts'
light up at dusk on Tara Boulevard,
red neon scribbling to the thundery air.

Goa

Even now I think of you with a kind of awe.
Do you laze this evening on an 'azure' shore,
you whom I last saw twenty years ago,
or contemplate from a beach house in Goa
the Indian Ocean breaking on the coast
where my love, gratitude and grief lie waste?
If only we'd fought off the final row;
but, poets both, we saw the drama through.
Decades divide us from the life we lost
and only in spirit can I be with you now.

Art Notes

I A LIGHTHOUSE IN MAINE

— Edward Hopper

It might be anywhere, that ivory tower
reached by a country road. Granite and sky,
it faces every which way with an air
of squat omniscience, intensely mild,
a polished Buddha figure warm and dry
beyond vegetation; and the sunny glare
striking its shingled houses is no more
celestial than the hot haze of the world.

Built to shed light but also hoarding light,
it sits there dozing in the afternoon
above the ocean like a ghostly moon
patiently waiting to illuminate.
You make a left beyond the town, a right,
you turn a corner and there, ivory-white,
it shines in modest glory above a bay.
Out you get and walk the rest of the way.

2 THE REALM OF LIGHT

— René Magritte

The picture in the picture window shows
an aspen, is it, a house calm and clear
at dawn or dusk, a lamp post's yellow light
abuzz on shutters and a shivering pond.
Aspen and roof aspire though, point beyond
the upstairs reading lamp to another sphere
where, behind deckled leaves, pacific rows
of cloud file slowly past, serenely white.

It must be dusk, with the light almost gone,
but view this picture with extreme distrust
since what you see is the *trompe-l'oeil* of dream.
It *might* be dusk, with the house almost dead;
or is there somebody getting out of bed,
the exhausted street light anxious for a rest,
birds waking in the trees, the clouds astream
in an invisible breeze? It must be dawn.

3 STUDIO IN ANTIBES

— Nicolas de Staël

'Waiting on chance to get the pictures out
otherwise locked in the chromatic brain,
I've worked the nerves into a curious state,
talk only to my models and sleep alone.
Je sais que ma solitude est inhumaine.
Here I renounce abstraction, turning again
to the world of objects, to the stoical souls
of candlesticks and jugs, bottles and bowls.

'After the blue nudes the attentive studio
fills up again with coffee, bread and fruit,
with sun and sky, white gulls in sudden flight
when I open the window on a misty night,
rocks and a lighthouse, fishing boats in port;
but paint can't give me what I need to know.
A yellow concert starts up in my head,
soon growing in volume as it turns to red.'

4 CUSHENDUN IN WINTER

— Maurice Wilks

North light on the snowlight on a little bridge
where once we loitered during a previous age
in the quiet dusk of one more summer day
as the sun went down behind the Antrim hills
and Scotland dimly shone across the water.
Girls watched the boys go by, the boys the girls,
the Lavery sisters and the postman's daughter;
later we'd flirt with them at Lynn's Café.

Wilks never bothered with 'the picture plane',
with 'colour values' and the fancy words —
as for aesthetics, that was for the birds.
They slept in a yellow trailer at Shane's Cairn
where, every morning, he would paint the world:
hedges, fields, the sunlight on the river,
the forest and the dunes, a still unspoiled
paradise we thought would last for ever.

5 BIRDS

— Georges Braque

(after Saint-John Perse)

The swift plunge of the artist, raptor and rapt,
seizes them in a flash and flings them down
on the lithographic plate, there to be shaped
for the sky-page, printed though never trapped;
their brows those of dolphins or the newborn,
gathered like ghosts, unmindful of their own
shadows, they fly to their remote wing songs
leaving us silent in the bronze of gongs.

Day being too short for them, they cruise at night.
Stripped for action, slick as spacecraft, driven
by two strokes to the spectral limits of flight,
they move like language to a cosmic rhythm,
like wind-blown paper, leaves or tongues of flame.
Blurring the moon, they glide down tracts of time;
abstracted from the facts and lost to sight,
they save for us something of the creative dream.

6 RAIN

— Howard Hodgkin

Some kind of board and an old frame will do
for his strong hues and open brush strokes.
This sodden emerald, this windswept blue
roaring into the back yard, oil on wood,
are representational though not wholly so
being largely 'about paint' and the residue
of primitive alchemy in the dreamworks:
he'd make gold in a piss-pot if he could.

Bombay is a pretext for hot yellow and brown
where a tandoori sun has just gone down;
the lovers, a frank swirl of head-to-head
organic shapes, are ginger on gland-red,
two spicy colours making violent love;
and the long breakers in a briny cove
streaming exultantly on the bread board
are black and blue come quick into their own.

7 WAVE SHADOW

— Vivienne Roche

Of glass and bronze, it gasps and faintly heaves,
cascading down like rain or up like leaves
in a light breeze, and rippling ridges hear
a chattering atrium or an echoing pool
with its clinical, brain-rinsing atmosphere.
You could float here for ever, blue and cool,
waves sloshing round the details that refer
sidelong to Hokusai, to Neolithic caves

and the blue dolphins in Ariadne's bedroom
chuckling and diving up there even now.
Wave theory liberates the ebb and flow:
where will the drip drop or the foam form,
what dim considerations move the cloud?
What more in heaven and in the sea below?
A gleaming boardwalk bridges the divide
from raw experience to the other side.

8 SAVANNAH DOCK

— Anthony Palliser

(*for Diane*)

There you are, coming from your wooden wharf
as if in a photograph or a home movie.
Perhaps you've been for a swim, a lazy sail
on the great river, 'wider than a mile',
or out to sea to where the Gullah live
in their sea islands and the heavy surf,
a thundering ocean, throws up African stuff.
The sun is shining and you look lovely.

The green light at the end of Daisy's dock
and Gatsby's crazy parties at Great Neck
are worlds away from your own natural space
where an unmeretricious real moon shines
and stars are mild above the Georgia pines.
May life be gentle in your scented air
and the art flourish that you nourish there
in peace and quiet, far from the marketplace.

9 TRIPTYCH

(for Anne Madden)

Pompeiian door frames, crimson and ultramarine
air boxes choking with black smoke and ash
blow clear to sea light like a tambourine.
The sun's forge, a gold continuous crash,
roars and flickers with perpetual flames;
winged figures circulate in the airstreams
and an ill-fated one, having flown too high,
drops into legend through a whirling sky.

Hang-gliding in the sun like Saint-Exupéry
the hawk or lapwing, a brave girl or boy,
dives to the gravitational field of the sea,
one tiny lifeboat like an abandoned toy
or its own shadow: picture the climax though,
the wild euphoria when for a minute or so,
deaf to the crackling kite tackle of gravity,
it flaps there treading air in a hot glow.

Space-time is a spun network where it falls
to a dash of paint and graphite, inks and oils,
dense atmospherics, bright transparencies.
Night comes with cloudy hands, the windy skies
are 'filled with graves', but a night garden fills
with moonlit palms, cicadas, murmuring souls;
blue-white and luminous in a partial dark,
your stairs lead up to the calm house of work.

Research

An actual conch
like a human head on its side,
washed up and left here by the ebb tide,
a magical sculpture, perfectly arbitrary,
lies as if dropped from orbit.
Oh, they will launch

research to find
ice in the Sea of Rains,
a first dubious twitch of mud and plants,
signs of life on the other planets,
whispers of inchoate mind
and flickering brains.

Meanwhile on Earth
we've mud, plants, pleasure, pain
and even real lives to be getting on with;
seasons for this and that, the works and days
of many mice and men
as Hesiod says.

Best to ignore
'the great ocean of truth',
the undiscovered seas of outer space,
and research this real unconscious conch on the shore
with its polished, archaic face
and its air of myth.

A Country Road

Long live the weeds and the wilderness yet.
— Hopkins

Above rising crops
the sun peeps like an eclipse
in a snow of hawthorn, and a breeze sings
its simple pleasure in the nature of things,
a tinkling ditch and a long field
where tractors growled.

Second by second
cloud swirls on the globe as though
political; lilacs listen to the wind,
watching birds circle in the yellow glow
of a spring day, in a sea stench
of kelp and trench.

Are we going to laugh
on the road as if the whole
show was set out for our grand synthesis?
Abandoned trailers sunk in leaves and turf,
slow erosion, waves on the boil . . .
We belong to this —

not as discrete
observing presences but as born
participants in the action, sharing of course
'the seminal substance of the universe'
with hedgerow, flower and thorn,
rook, rabbit and rat.

These longer days
bursting with sunlit fruit
and some vague confidence inspire besides
skittish bacteria, fungi, viruses, gastropods
squirming in earth and dirt.
Dark energies,

resisting gravity,
fling farther the red-shifting gas
but the lone bittern and the red grouse,
crying 'Go back!', have got the measure of it.
Animal, vegetable, mineral watch
as we walk their patch;

and a bath in the woods,
its brown depths where once
a bubbling foam of soap and juniper.
Now tar water of Cloyne, cow faces, clouds,
ice of the winter months
and nobody there.

Nobody there
for days and nights but our own
curious thoughts in a storm or before dawn.
Bird, beast and flower, whatever your names are,
like the wind blowing through
we belong here too.

Homage to Gaia

I ITS RADIANT ENERGIES

A world of dikes and bikes
   where yoghurt weavers drive
on gin and margarine . . .
   This is how to live

in the post-petroleum age,
   gathering light-beams
to run the house with clean
   photoelectric frames

that trap the sun and focus
   its radiant energies;
their glow reflects the seasons,
   cloud cover, open skies.

Our micro-climate gives us
   gentle winters here.
Spring starts in January
   and lasts throughout the year

with its perennial flowers,
   so even an average annual
thousand kilowatt hours
   per photovoltaic panel

looks feasible in time.
   What you notice about
the panes is their composure,
   their heliotropic quiet

as star-gazing, rain-laced,
   light-drinking polysilicon
raises its many faces
   to worship the hot sun.

Great sun, dim or bright,
    eye in the changing sky,
send us warmth and light!
    We can never die

while you are roaring there
    in serial rebirth
far from our atmosphere.
    Remember life on Earth!

2 HOMAGE TO GAIA

Since we destroyed the woods
  with crazy chainsaws, oiled
the sea, burned up the clouds,
  upset the natural world

to grow fat, if I may
  I want to apologize
for our mistakes and pay
  homage to seas and skies,

to field and stream; to you,
  great Gaia our first mother
with your confused retinue
  of birds, your weird weather.

You've done so much for us
  and what do we give back?
Suspension bridges, yes,
  and columns of black smoke.

Blowing hot and cold,
  you love us and hate us both;
we babble about the world
  while you sustain the earth.

You will prevail of course
  if in a different form;
we go from bad to worse
  just trying to keep warm.

3 WIND AND WAVE

Quixote would pick a fight
   with wind turbines, more
bad giants gesticulating
   from onshore and offshore —

not realizing that these
   and the far-sighted wave
fetching up from long
   seas with a final heave

transform the wild energies
   of chaos and old night
into a clean and infinite
   source of power and light.

Coleridge kept an Aeolian
   harp like a harmonica
lodged in an open window
   to catch the slightest flicker

of even the faintest breeze
   in even the calmest weather,
the Muse of music dozing
   upon her quiet zither —

for this is the true breath
   of life, the air that sings
in larynx and sea froth
   and ruffles the spread wings;

this is the wind that drives
   the dark waves below
to light our homely lives
   with an unearthly glow.

Blow, wind, and seize
    the slick rotors! Race,
tide, to the estuaries
    so we shine on in space!

4 SAND AND STARS

The night life of the shore:
   rock music, flashing light.
Increasingly I prefer
   to get an early night;

yet here I am, listening
   again to a cold strand,
the vast sky glistening
   like blown dust or sand.

Ancient shingle races,
   clicking and sparkling, down
to wild watery chaos.
   As for the twinkly town,

roofed like a sea surface
   with moonlit tiles, the eye
measures its tiny houses
   against an enormous sky.

Gardens find their right
   higher and lower levels;
rockeries stagger out
   like underwater shelves.

High tide among the pines,
   cod caves in the boughs,
plaice flap in the ruins
   of sunken bungalows.

5 AT URSULA'S

A cold and stormy morning.
      I sit in Ursula's place
and fancy something spicy
      served with the usual grace

by one of her bright workforce
      who know us from before,
a nice girl from Cracow,
      Penang or Baltimore.

Some red basil linguine
      would surely hit the spot,
something light and shiny,
      mint-yoghurty and hot;

a frosty but delightful
      pistachio ice-cream
and some strong herbal
      infusion wreathed in steam.

Once a tomato sandwich
      and a pint of stout would do
but them days are over.
      I want to have a go

at some amusing fusion
      Thai and Italian both,
a dish of squid and pine nuts
      simmered in lemon broth,

and catch the atmospherics,
      the happy lunchtime crowd,
as the cold hand gets warmer
      and conversation loud.

Boats strain at sea, alas,
gales rattle the slates
while inside at Ursula's
we bow to our warm plates.

6 LONDON RAIN

It raps at the skylights
   of Soho flats, a vast
vertical downpour long
   awaited, here at last

panicking car alarms,
   making the windows gleam
and rinsing hot roof tiles
   in clouds of rising steam.

It hoses the back doors
   of the very first high-rise
car park in London
   where I've checked for days

on the speaking, anachronistic
   fate of a paint blister
scraped and flaking into
   a heap of dust and plaster.

Buses and taxis thrash
   under a thundery sky,
tracking down Regent St.
   'To shops in crowds' they fly

as if from an air-raid
   in the strange early dark.
Rain falls like space debris
   on Brick Lane, Hyde Park,

St Paul's and Primrose Hill,
   streams down as it used to do
for whole hours at a stretch
   on evenings long ago.

But this is a new rain
   the rainmakers have sent,
corporate and imported
   to swamp a continent.

Earthquake and tsunami!
   Wasteful and cackling, Thames
water still bubbles away
   as in more temperate times.

Euphoric as it crashes
   riotously from the tap,
it still flows and twinkles
   as if it will never stop —

even when a rainbow drips
   above Bayswater, the sky turns
to a glistening denim-blue
   and an evening star shines.

Think of this abundance
   when the bright splatter blows
eastwards, leaving the heavens
   a washed-out yellow-rose.

7 ODE TO BJÖRK

Dark bird of ice, dark swan
   of snow, your bright gamine
teardrop Inuit eyes
   peep from a magazine

as if to say 'Fuck off
   and get my new release;
you don't know *me*, I am
   the dark swan of ice

and secrecy, the seagull,
   the unringed plover, not
something to tame and stroke.'
   Ever since Spit & Snot,

'Aeroplane' and 'Anchor Song'
   your aim has been to knock
aside the expectations
   of corporate brainwash rock.

'Headphones' and 'Cover Me',
   I listen to your voice,
a lonely bird that pipes
   from quickly thawing ice,

a bad child acting out
   behind the electronics,
a mad flirt and shout
   beyond the audio mix.

No doubt you'd like to get
   an open car, a megaphone
and tell the world like Garbo
   'I want to be alone!'

Here in the confused stink
    of global warming what
you really want, I think,
    is not spit 'n' snot

but mystery and mystique,
    the hidden places where
the wild things are and no one
    can track you to your lair.

(Sea levels rising annually,
    glaciers sliding fast,
species extinct, the far north
    negotiable at last . . .)

Anyhow you're not playing
    to us, are you, but to the white
light and corrugated iron
    roofs of the Arctic night.

Up there where silence falls
    and there is no more land
your scared, scary voice calls
    to the great waste beyond.

8 DIRIGIBLES

We who used to drift
    superbly in mid-air,
each a giant airship
    before 'the last war',

shrink to a soft buzz
    above financial centres
surprising visitors,
    hackers and bean counters

in cloud-flown high-rises.
    Cloud-slow, we snoop for hours
on open-plan offices
    and cloudy cocktail bars.

Amnesia and mystique
    have cast into oblivion
fiery failures like
    Italia, R101,

the whole brief catalogue
    of mad catastrophes;
and showy *Hindenburg*
    of course, the last of these.

A temporary setback.
    Our time will come again
with helium in the sack
    instead of hydrogen

while slow idealists
    gaze at refrozen ice,
reflourishing rain forests,
    the oceans back in place;

at sand and stars, blue skies,
    clear water, scattered light
as in the early days
    of nearly silent flight.

9 AN INDIAN GARDEN

Indigo night fronds like
   quills dipped in ink
share in the life cycle
   as quietly they drink

the close tropical heat.
   New coconuts take shape
in clusters out of reach,
   'patrimony of the ape'

said Durrell. A well-aimed
   machete stroke; you sip
nectar, and the brainy
   skull is its own cup.

It rots in sandy soil
   here at the ocean rim,
changing to coal and oil
   through geological time.

The spiritual substance
   we generate likewise
rejoins the ancient dance.
   It never really dies

but circulates at random
   somewhere in the ether
when body closes down;
   and so we live for ever.

Turtle Beach

Black laterite outcrops ranged along
the seaboard shield them from the most
alarming feature of this coast,
mud chaos of the rainy months —
but not from parties, thong and song,
when the new people dance the dance.

The crow and the high Brahminy kite
know about the amphibious chicks
due to emerge on hatching night
and flipper-scramble down the shore.
The toughs are up to their old tricks,
looking out for a chance to score;

but still the turtles once a year
head for nest sites up the beach:
the human footprint doesn't scare
these creatures from their sanctuary.
Only night-sight cameras watch
the young in their wild dash to the sea.

Goa

Homage to Goa

The ceiling fans in the house go round and round
as if to whisk us off to a different sky.
I squirt Deet at a thin mosquito whine;
gods chuckle softly from a garden shrine,
fruit ripen in the gloaming without a sound.
Parvati, Shiva, Ganesh the elephant boy
promote the comical to the sublime; though, shown
a choice of deities, I defer like most
to violet Krishna in the heat and dust,
brother of Dionysus, expert in everything —
flute-player, hero and lecher, comedian, king.

I rock on a warm verandah as daylight goes.
The hippies too revered him in the old days
of hair and beads, torchlight and astro trance,
trailing from poppy field to lamasery
as irksome and imperious as Camões.
It's snowing in Kashmir, but here in Goa
we already have spring temperatures. Anandu
waters the earth and brushes up the sand.
Banana leaves and plantains in a daze
trade oxygen for tar; *tat tvam asi*.
Already a heavy mango strikes the ground.

A mozzie once myself, *I* buzzed and bit —
but only foot and elbow, ear and knee;
a cheeky monkey keen on human thought,
with a reach greater than my grasp, I'd dance
wildly at times, conscious of ignorance,
or chew on my own morose inadequacy.
Still, I behaved, and so the next time out
I got to sit to a half-mad sadhu
at Brahmin school. 'The body is a shadow,'
said he, 'it tells you in the Upanishads';
but spirit knows no slapstick or romance.

The clouds recycle and we spread like plants,
waves smash on beaches for no obvious purpose
except to deliver the down-to-earth palingenesis
of multitudinous life particles. A porpoise
revolves on the sky as if in outer space
where we started out so many aeons ago.
Goa fact file: infant mortality low,
average life expectancy seventy-five,
functional literacy sixty-nine percent;
the porcupine and flying fox survive,
also the sloth bear and shy Chital doe.

'The streaming meteor, is it dead or alive,
a deliberate thing or merely gas and stone?
Some believe in a life after this one
while others say we're only nut and leaf.
An ageing man repents his wicked ways:
we began so innocently, and may again'
— Abu al-Ma'ari, 10th century, Syrian.
Given a choice between paradise and this life
I'd choose this life with its calamities,
the shining sari, the collapsing wave,
the jeep asleep beneath the coconut trees.

Skyflower, flame-of-the-forest among the palms,
ripe mangoes dropping from the many limbs,
the radio twang of a high-pitched sitar,
'Kareena Kapoor in Hot New Avatar'!
A gecko snaps a spider from a window.
Given a choice of worlds, here or beyond,
I'd pick this one not once but many times
whether as mozzie, monkey or pure mind.
The road to enlightenment runs past the house
with its auto-rickshaws and its dreamy cows
but the fans, like the galaxies, go round and round.

Ithaca

As promised, the Corfu crew put him ashore
at dawn, still dozing, where the sea's roar
turned in his ears, and so he woke at last
on his own soil. Athene threw a sea mist
over the rocks, and after many a year
he didn't know his native earth at first.
'Oh, not *another* island!', he complained.
'Whose meadows are those above the strand?
Will they be primitive and barbarian
or civilized people who will take me in?
Those damn swindlers promised a clear run
to Ithaca, and instead they've set me down
in a strange place I never saw before.'
So musing, lost and bored but still alive,
he gathered up the gear and made his way
along the cold edge of the hissing sea,
up sandy paths, past lemon and wild olive.
'Sir,' said Athene of the shining eyes,
'you must be far gone not to recognize
a famous country known to east and west,
from where the sun rises to where it sets.
It boasts fine pasture for cows and goats,
oak, pine and boatyards. It's not vast,
as you will see, but rich in crops and wine
and generously fed with dew and rain.
I always knew you'd make it in the end —
and here you are, although without your men.
Yes, this is Ithaca, and there's the shrine
to your belovèd wood nymphs.' The sea mist
cleared, and the countryside lay all around.
Astonished at the sight of his own island
— 'Ithaca!' — he raised a pious hand
and spoke to the familiar shrine: 'Receive
my prayer, a prayer of gratitude and love.
I will bring gifts again as in the past
if great Athene lets me live to taste
the joys of home, relinquished years ago,

and sit down with my family once more.'
'Our first task,' said Athene, 'is to stow
your gold and bronzes in the sacred cave
and then decide on where we go from there.'

Blueprint

The gardeners are already waiting.
— Brecht

Trucks from New Jersey (fruit and veg),
panting beneath the window ledge
and drowning out the twitter-cheep
of sparrows on the fire escape,
start up the mad Manhattan day.
The sun, coming the other way,
glitters on offices and planes,
on Jeep, Dodge and commuter trains

streaming from bridge and tunnel mouth,
from out of town, from north and south.
At shark time in the market, though,
some slacker on the Hudson piers
or quiet, tree-lined avenue,
inactive at mid-morning, hears
a different music of the spheres
from what the corporate buzzards know.

There *was* a blueprint from the past
but scribbled on by guilty pens
till it was virtually effaced.
Now, slowly running down despite
what the best economic brains
devise, the culture's clinging tight
to its 'full-spectrum dominance' —
friend and destroyer, both at once.

'Clearance Sale', 'Everything Must Go':
with homeless folks and unemployed
growing in number day and night,
the gritty streets begin to look
as they did eighty years ago
in the old pictures; and it took

another war to put that right
and start us on the upward slide.

Out there in a great plain or wood
a leaf unfolds the rolling news
mutation writes, and the wind sighs
secrets the ancients understood.
Enough, already, with the failed
agendas; give the Algonquin back
the shiny vein of ore we struck
and watch them re-enchant the world!

A Quiet Spot

We tire of cities in the end:
the whirr and blur of it, so long your friend,
grows repetitious and you start to choke
on signage, carbon monoxide, the hard look.
You always knew it would come down
to a dozy seaside town —

not really in the country, no,
but within reach of the countryside,
somewhere alive to season, wind and tide,
far field and wind farm. 'Wrong life,' said Adorno,
'can't be lived rightly.' The right place
is a quiet spot like this

where an expanding river spills,
still trout-rich, from the dewy hills
of Cork, still fertile in a morning mist.
So, do you pause to congratulate yourself
out here at the continental shelf,
far from the hysteria,

on the perfect work-life balancing act
you've found after so many a fugitive year
of travel? If so, let the pause be brief.
Gaia demands your love, the patient earth
your airy sneakers tread expects
humility and care.

It's time now to go back at last
beyond irony and slick depreciation,
past hedge and fencing to a clearer vision,
time to create a future from the past,
tune out the babbling radio waves
and listen to the leaves.

The Thunder Shower

A blink of lightning, then
a rumour, a grumble of white rain
growing in volume, rustling over the ground,
drenching the gravel in a wash of sound.
Drops tap like timpani or shine
like quavers on a line.

It rings on exposed tin,
a suite for water, wind and bin,
plinky Poulenc or strongly groaning Brahms'
rain strings, a whole string section that describes
the very shapes of thought in warm
self-referential vibes

and spreading ripples. Soon
the whispering roar is a recital.
Jostling rain crowds, clamorous and vital,
struggle in runnels through the afternoon.
The rhythm becomes a regular beat;
steam rises, body heat —

and now there's city noise,
bits of recorded pop and rock,
the drums, the strident electronic shock,
a vast polyphony, the dense refrain
of wailing siren, truck and train
and incoherent cries.

All human life is there
in the unconfined, continuous crash
whose slow, diffused implosions gather up
car radios and alarms, the honk and beep,
and tiny voices in a crèche
piercing the muggy air.

Squalor and decadence,
the rackety global-franchise rush,

oil wars and water wars, the diatonic
crescendo of a cascading world economy
are audible in the hectic thrash
of this luxurious cadence.

The voice of Baal explodes,
raging and rumbling round the clouds,
frantic to crush the self-sufficient spaces
and reimpose his failed hegemony
in Canaan before moving on
to other simpler places.

At length the twining chords
run thin, a watery sun shines out,
the deluge slowly ceases, the guttural chant
subsides; a thrush sings, and discordant thirds
diminish like an exhausted concert
on the subdominant.

The angry downpour swarms
growling to far-flung fields and farms.
The drains are still alive with trickling water,
a few last drops drip from a broken gutter;
but the storm that created so much fuss
has lost interest in us.

New Space

Swept and scrubbed, the studio fills
with cut cloth, illustrated books,
materials shaped by polished skills
in a time-honoured fashion, one
that aims for a real thing well done
with real significance. Just look

at how green light and shadow fall
on the interior, jug and bowl,
still life, *nature morte*. The place
itself is a still life restored
to living matter, a new space
whose true life is renewed once more.

A coach house in equestrian days,
it makes one with the vegetable
garden beyond the ceramic glaze
inside and the converted stable
loft where an old record plays
to pram and pine and summer breeze.

It's all the one, the clay, the cloth,
art, music and organic growth
nursing the venerable ideal
of spirit lodged within the real.
Tolstoy, who later disapproved
of opera, plays and novels, loved

doorknobs, utensils, toys and song,
the homespun that the peasants wore —
everything simple, strong and clean,
art that was modest, not a chore;
and rhyming verses, not too long,
that say exactly what they mean.

Though the sun rises in a blaze
these mornings, breaking up the haze,

I'm less in love with the sublime,
more interested in the neat rows
laid out to raise the beans and peas,
rosemary, parsley, sage and thyme.

The weight of a bone-handled knife
signifies more in human life
than our aesthetics ever can;
form follows function. Once again
we look to the still living whole
to heal the heart and cure the soul.

Air India

(Delhi-Heathrow)

A haughty camel train in the rush hour,
a holy cow chewing a cardboard box,
sand-thudding fruit, a dusty star —
these are the images that recur,
and the new office blocks.

Sand-scraping branches making *namaskar*
to the brown sea from a 'Bounty'-wrapper beach,
a nipper's goofy toy inflatable shark,
idle kites circling a railway bridge,
old Delhi after dark;

a woodsmoke evening, the pink architecture,
moth-fluttering crowds around the sanctuary
where six-branched Shiva sits like a gilt candlestick,
some hunched-up creature watching
the sunrise from a cedar tree . . .
But the clearest picture

is a weed-trailing yard of wood and brick
up a dim lane behind a bicycle shop
with a quick monkey, rhesus or macaque,
clinging for dear life to a water pipe,
the slowly dripping tap.

World Trade Talks

Downturn Means CO$_2$ Targets Now Achievable

A 'Hindu' growth rate,
hedges against the winds
of double-edged finance; organic crops
and comely maidens, is it too late
to push for these demands
and pious hopes?

The great Naomi Klein
condemns, in *The Shock Doctrine*,
the Chicago Boys, the World Bank and the IMF,
the dirty tricks and genocidal mischief
inflicted upon the weak
who now fight back.

A hare in the corn
scared by the war machine
and cornered trembling in its exposed acre,
a sacred thing projected on the moon
when the full moon is clear,
survives the roar

by lying low
in the heart-withering breeze.
Next spring, when a new crop begins to grow,
let it not be genetically modified
but such as the ancients sowed
in the old days.

Ash and Aspen

Their captive spirits groan as one
with a new yearning to be free
of the old fate, the old constraints —
faint whispers of conspiracy
from hazel, juniper and birch
shaking arthritic finger joints,
keening together each alone
in unison. Which witch is which?

Wide, oval mouths of agèd ash
vowel their bondage; stricken hands
and keys articulate their anguish.
They are committed root and branch
and dream of flight to no avail,
shrinking to rigid furniture,
table and wardrobe, desk and chair,
everything 'Antaeus-like'. Meanwhile

the aspen whistles fast and loud
with forecast and astonishment,
light heart and breezy equinoxes.
Oceans rustle in the strings
of this celestial instrument.
Its shiny paper pours like wings
of inspiration; the soft wood
is used for matches and matchboxes.

Growth

The gardens have survived the ice
that laid the country bare and clear,
their grasses rising fast and fierce
through splintered water, frosty air,
soft swords reclaiming heritage
from squeaking mud and creaking ditch.

After the dawn commuters leave
in the Range Rovers, four by four,
the quiet of an hour's reprieve
except on a few building sites.
The global oil-price crisis bites;
an April mist lifts from the shore.

Not 'rock and thorn' but field and wood
slope to the sea below the town.
The tree stands where it always stood,
a knuckly oak beside the spring
reaching skywards like a druid,
firm in its place and flourishing.

The secret source still running clean
of brick dust and detergent froth
that wither so much natural growth,
the woodpigeon, the thrush and wren
hide in the branches to discharge
soul music to the world at large.

Quercus petraea, Dair ghaelach —
sunlight smokes in its archaic
antlers and visceral mistletoe.
Old oak of Durrow and Kildare!
The leaves reflect a golden glow;
no lightning strike has crackled there.

The Seasons

(for Matthew Geden)

1

Day-stars like daisies on a field of sky.
The nuclear subs are keeping sinister watch
while sun heat focuses on the cabbage patch.
What weird weather can we expect this July?
Tornado, hail, some sort of freak tempest?
The bonfire month, *and another storm brewing:*
I hear it sing i' th' wind, and among the leaves.
But out here in the hot pastures of the west,
no Google goggling at our liminal lives,
there are still corners where a lark can sing.

2

We prospered and made hay while the sun shone.
Now autumn skies, yellow and grey, sow rain
on summer debris, *Ambre Solaire*, crushed bracken,
we clear the dead leaves from a blocked drain
and tap barometers since the weather's taken
a sudden turn for the worse. Contentious crows
congregate of an evening at St Multose';
the harvest hymns float out from Gothic windows
on Maersk, docked sailing-boats and guesthouses
closed for the winter now the guests have gone.

3

The reading period, and on the writing desk
quarto and lamplight in the early dusk.
If we don't travel now we hibernate
with other locals at the Tap Tavern
beside an open hearth, our winter haven.
Glowing cinders nuzzle the warm grate
while outside, ghostly in a starlit street,

creaking signs and a novelistic breeze.
Urgent footsteps fade into the night
leaving us to our pub talk and reveries.

4

A fly-dazzling disc in the open door,
hung on a ribbon, catches light and blinks
as the sun spokes on gardens and seascapes,
drawing up dew, exposing hidden depths,
old shipwrecks visible from the air. A northern
draught blows flower scents to the blue horizon;
a yawl, Bermuda-rigged, shakes out its linen
watched by the yachties, blow-ins, quiet drunks
and the new girls with parasols in their drinks.
Springs gush in a shower of flowering hawthorn.

After the Storm

After the storm a tentative blackbird chorus,
silent throughout it, started cheeping again.
The city, for fear of a worse overflow,
had unlocked dams, so water levels rose
at an alarming rate; the rivers burst
their banks, swamping fields in a sea of rain,
and flooded low-lying districts in one go,
the waters sparing neither man nor beast.
Square miles shrank as a sudden deluge rushed
from the rain-sodden hills. *Ye nymphes of Bandon*,
where were you when the great south-facing windows
of heaven were opened and it bucketed down
on quiet Munster? No one had imagined
embankments would give way under the surge,
the River Lee engulfing market towns'
water mains, drains and residential lanes.
It struck in late November, so by and large
no ripening crops suffered, no standing grain,
but haylofts were awash and much of the hard
work of the summer proved to be in vain.
Reservoirs, lakes poured down in a tide of mud
submerging farms. An astonishing six inches
fell in a single night from inky cloud.
Not much distinction now between sea and land:
some sat in dinghies rowing where they'd sown,
navigating their own depth-refracted ground
and scaring salmon from among the branches.
Global warming, of course, but more like war
as if dam-busting bombers had been here:
aerial photographs of the worst-hit areas
showed roads, bridges, basic infrastructure
devastated, the kind of thing you expect
in India or China but not in Cork.
Detritus of the years, carpet and car,
computers and a wide range of expensive
gadgetry went spinning down the river
with furniture and linen, crockery, shoes

and clothes, until it finally gave over;
not everyone had full insurance cover.
The inquiry dealt only with technical issues,
avoiding larger questions. Telephone
lines down, 'Boil Water' notices in force,
drainage schemes overwhelmed and of no use,
authorities hinted that it could've been worse.
(There would be building work for months to come,
developers would have no cause to complain.)
A general cleaning-up operation began;
houses, garages, skips gleamed with the slime
deposited everywhere like a disease.
We will get over it though we're not sure how.
The country sighed in the calm after the storm,
emergency services got to grips with the grim
sequel as drowned townlands emerged at last,
the earth increasing as the flow decreased.
The birds, crowing and piping with relief,
announced a partial return to normal life
and light shone in the cloud until next time.
It's snow and black ice we've to contend with now.

Beached Whale

Snow from the north, hail, and a ruffled gull
rises from cold dunes at break of day
when the shore belongs to the gale,
the frozen algae and the beached whale
fluke-thrashing as she breathes her dying
breaths and gradually subsides
under the great weight of her own insides.

The transatlantic dash was nothing to her,
a fine finback, her notion of a trip
some new dimension, gravity defied,
the dive at dusk through the empyrean
whooping and chuckling in her slick and drip,
stinking and scooping up the fry,
rusty and barnacled like an old steamship.

On moonlit nights her bubbling orifices
dribbled for miles, mysterious and capricious,
where she went spouting, eerie as Moby Dick,
far from the known sea lanes, her whistle and click
distinguishable from Cape Clear to Cape Race;
on a calm day she'd snooze
exposed and ruminant on the sunny surface.

Out of her depth now, her rorqual pleats
ivory fading to grey as the tide retreats,
her brain at rest, with her huge size
she has admirers in her drowsy eyes —
surfers and tourists, children, families
who never saw a whale before;
and the news cameras, RTÉ, Channel 4.

A tired eye closes after so many years,
so much experience, travel, league upon league
of ocean, wild sunrises and sunsets,
tropical storms, long vistas, wind and stars;
and she gives up the ghost

not in the unfathomable dark forest
of sea, but here on the strand at Timoleague.

Pliny thought dolphins beached for love of man,
aspiring to human life. A mighty beast
like this has other reasons (pheromone,
exhaustion, age), yet when she gasps her last
bad breath on the glassy sand she gives
her body to flensing knives
and the flesh falls away in heavy leaves —

source once of lamp oil, glue and candle grease.
Dead of some strange respiratory disease,
reduced to the ribcage of an old wreck,
entrails strewn on mud, the stomach
stripped and the organs — heart, liver
and lights — retrieved for research,
she knows we aim to make a study of her;

to study the cortex, the skin thick and thin,
her ancient knowledge of the seas and rocks
we left to climb up on the burning shore
and still revisit in dreams and sex,
where the soft human paw
has the reflex of an unthinking fin
or a nerve twitching in primordial depths.

At the Butler Arms

No boats this week, too choppy, so we watch
from a spread table beneath
a Charlie Chaplin photograph
who often came here for a holiday;
or we drive over to Finian's Cove to study
the eight-mile stretch

of water between here and Sceilig Mhichíl
where the old anchorites
and monks who chose the place and raised
a church, two chapels and six drystone huts,
survived on dulse and mackerel
out in the haze.

No pleasant woodland there, no grazing deer
such as the others knew
above fly-bubbling salmon streams ashore,
in field and forest beneath oak and yew —
not calm, contemplative ease
but violent seas.

Six hundred years of plainchant and response,
gannet and cormorant; six
centuries of the 'crude bronze crucifix'
in Finian's church, wine cup and canticle,
prayer book and reading candle,
thistles, sea campions.

How could you get inside their bony heads?
Wrapped up in mystic mists,
they spent the hours and years
wrestling with the hot flesh in their cold beds,
their backs to Europe and the wars,
talking to ghosts.

What news of the great world, of Gaul and Rome,
Iona and Cappadocia? Some,

but late; prostrate at Easter in the nave
they listened to the whistling wave
and saw the sun sink in an infinite ocean
world of its own.

Strong winds continue, so no trip this time.
Still, it could be predictable to climb
to the immense height and the whole shocking
reach of the Atlantic (with special care
since there's no handrail there).
No going back,

is there, to that wild hush of dedication,
to the solitude, the intense belief,
the last rock of an abandoned civilization
whose dim lights glimmered in a distant age
to illuminate at the edge
a future life.

Synge Dying

I didn't start it exactly but I was among
the first with bike and camera
to visit the wilder shores
of Kerry and Connemara
in search of old reality, stories,
folklore and traditional song.
I even introduced the clock to Aran.

Not real to myself, a sick man fighting for life
in the fey breezes and raw winds,
I was in two minds
about my right to be there
writing up the rough holy ground,
the roads, the *céilí* and the hiring fair.

But there in words I found
the living world I couldn't share;
now from the pillows
my gaze travels
past smoking chimneys to the distant hills.

A Building Site

Exposed dorms and corridors
squeak under the tracks
of cranes and earth-movers
and a fast shower rakes
the shattered greenhouses.

The school, a living surge
of nuns, skirts, blazers
and aprons, saw religion
take wing and fly away;
the site's a *tabula rasa*.

Of the old convent nothing
remains on this dark day.
New people in the prescribed
yellow protective clothing
string razor wire; from one

bare room to the next
the dangling terminals
and boxes of fresh bricks.
Beneath sliding skies
the new flats will rise.

One more dour complaint
at plywood and cement?
Certainly, though of course
perpetual change and flux
are the true element.

A grim summer, but if
fortuitous light strikes
the rubble and a sun-spoke
pierces a cloud rift
the meaning becomes clear.

The deconstruction here
— smashed tiles, splintered
wood, dismantled banisters,
tarpaulin and building gear
where once a convent stood —

opens a special place,
a field of rough energy
suspended for a minute
not at an 'interface'
or even a 'cutting edge'

but at a spinning centre
of heightened consciousness,
gives giddy glimpses into
a universe of blown
dust and distant stars.

This is the great answer
granted at a glance
and rained upon at once,
the magic coalition
of concrete circumstance —

the momentary, oblique
vision of an unknown
eternal dispensation,
the infinite republic
of primary creation.

Autumn Skies

I A DISTANT ECHO

Garvaghey, a 'rough field',
Dungannon and Armagh
remember the O'Neills
before the Tudor armies
trampled bog and sheugh.
We revel in that stuff —

still relevant enough
as our own new century
crushes the wild contours
of the ancestral dream.
Earth-movers champ and cough
at ancient glen and stream.

Same story everywhere,
the old Saint-Germain
market and Super Cannes
a corporate nightmare
while a bard holds aloof
under the leaking roof

of a dark house in Schull.
A killer roams the hills
but Muses mind with love
the hierophantic cave.
The *ceol mór* of long ago
lives on as a distant echo

drowned out by the noise
of ambient retail rock;
but a poet makes the soul
that only he can make
in a great singing school
of heather and wild dog rose.

2 A COUNTRY KITCHEN

'Walking into eternity'
along the breathing strand
there's that modality
immediately to hand —
spawn, wrack, far-out sea
and Howth Head beyond.

This is how it begins,
devotion to the real things
of a clean-swept morning:
leaf drip and birdsong,
work sounds, the rich
air of a country kitchen.

We toy with rhythm and rhyme
at a freshly lit hearth;
from under a close blanket
of ground fog the earth
opens up to a cloudstream
westwards in the Atlantic.

The world of simple fact
gleams with water, yields
to the plough. A gull race
follows the working tractor.
Quidditas: the used fields
of Ulster and ancient Greece;

and always the same river,
the oracle and universe
with no circumference,
that infinite resource.
If a thing happens once
it happens once for ever.

3 A QUIET COTTAGE

It all began at Inst.
You were among the finest
forwards in the great game
learning from the scrum
how to advance against
the exigencies of form.

'Think globally and act
locally': folk and jazz
sing to the autumn skies
and your creative tact.
Our cultural confusion
worked for resolution.

You found it in a quiet
cottage down the west
and took the answer back
to battered old Belfast;
bubbles of image smoke
rose from a chimney pot.

Guns under the floorboards,
cooped-up doves and pigeons
grumbled to the back yards
above belovèd motorbikes
in a city of rough politics
and murderous religions —

but the best thoughts survive
decades of hate and fear;
linen, cloud and snow
absorb the blood and tears.
Now we relax and live
the lives we used to know.

Earth voices in the branches,
butterflies at the flowers
on overgrown trenches,
and recent graves, replace
the historical nightmares.
Now we can die in peace.

Art and Reality

(for James Simmons, obiit 20/6/01)

Down white empty beaches my voice rang.

Jimmy, the harbour lights still shine
on Kerr St. and the railway line
from cold Portrush to cold Coleraine
and so to the great world; cold rain
still hammers into the West Strand
and the faint coast of Donegal,
the 'farther shore', the shining land
of childhood, fun and funeral.

Who would have thought you'd be the first
to quit the uproar of life's feast?
Barry's Amusements still go round;
the old Arcadia where once
the great Dave Glover and his band
played to your youthful innocence
still stands where the Atlantic knocks,
a pleasure dome above the rocks

that lost its neon sign long since.
The gulls still scream there on the roof
as if they miss your voice, as if
disconsolate for the cheery sight
of their blithe poet stepping out
in his trademark tweed overcoat —
a nonchalant rebel, *blasé*, bluff,
constantly singing, born to dance.

Burning the energy, burning up
the roads, not knowing when to stop,
every day was a rave and every
evening a new discovery.
Sworn to our tricky art, you chose
reality over art and pose —

357

an 'Honest Ulsterman' although
a rogue and romantic even so.

That title always bothered me,
the 'honest' claim seemed to imply
others were charlatans or worse:
we disagreed there at the start
one evening in the Longleys' house.
Perhaps reality and art,
grown disputatious, even thought
the two of them were poles apart

and not the mates they really are.
Oh, you could be a royal pain,
thorn in the side, flea in the ear.
Had you but *spar'd* your *tongue and pen*
you *might have rose like other men* —
though what's the point in 'rising' when
the kind of work we favoured thrives
in the night silence of the nerves?

When the guitars were packed away
and your Resistance Cabaret
took off into the sleeping town
planets and 'gaseous' sky looked down
on a dark province, brick and tile,
with cold indifference: not your style,
but didn't you tell it as it was?
'We're here because we're here because.'

You cherished girls of every age
and pitied the poor Paisleyite
deprived of your advantages.
Often your dodgy sexual ethic
emptied front rows; some splenetic
alderman would throw a tantrum.

Hillsborough, Portadown and Antrim
saw shocked audiences walk out.

We flinch, of course, when someone writes
our story by his different lights;
yet what I say agrees, I know,
with your self-estimate. We two
both wanted to help dissipate
the 'guilt and infantile self-hate',
each in his way, and find a voice
for the strange place bequeathed to us.

The hard men have renounced the gun
on *both* sides, you'd be glad to hear.
Two kinds of gullibles have begun,
hundreds of years too late, to share
the benefits; though, still unbowed,
we get around our psychic pain
by picking on the immigrant crowd:
we have disgraced ourselves again.

'Love what you can, die game,' you said —
and so you did, and so you did.
Your special genius found release
transporting the sad heart that longs
for new space and an open mind;
then you relinquished the old place
to sing on that white stretch of sand
in the distance. I still hum your songs.

Balcony of Europe

(for Aidan and Alannah Higgins)

The dictator's portrait dominated the airport
in those days, the first thing you noticed
after the cold police; his arms, a vivid
fistful of forked lightning, blazed
on the bus station and the road north-east
to the olive hills where the novelist lived.
The kitchen tap gave only a dry cough;
it was pitch black up there with the light off.

Down here at the sea-front forty years later,
on the *paseo*, at the Balcón de Europa bar
cameras, recorded accordion and guitar.
No shortage now of light or water,
everything so much brighter and better —
old wounds healed, old bones reconstituted;
and a young one in a swimsuit plays
on the shore as she did in ancient days

when she wasn't only a girl but a creature
of myth, a Phoenician king's abducted daughter
with a white bull between her knees,
borne out to a sun-white sea shaking with fear
and exhilaration far from her shocked sisters,
gripping the horns, clutching the curly hair,
et tremulae sinuantur flamine vestes
('her floaty garments fluttering in the breeze').

Under the Volcanoes

Todo se puede corregir.
>   — César Manrique, 1985

The heat seekers of Cork have been coming here
to Lanzarote year after solar year
in the high season, to sit on balconies
and bob like cork in the sub-tropical seas.
A cruise ship, bound for Europe, shimmers past
far out, its music system going full blast,
to join October in the temperate zones.
It's hereabouts, said Plato in *Timaeus*,
the lost Atlantis lies; and the Hesperides
retain their charm, even in these dark days.
The golden apples of the sun, of course,
are the great draw, and the rich local wines
uncorked as a red African disc swoons
into the western sea. The charcoal-black
volcanic sand, the cactus thick and coarse
in the dry scrub beyond the beaten track
make this a different kind of destination.
MacNeice chose Iceland for his holiday stuff
as if he couldn't ever get north enough —
but the Cork crowd, weary of fog and rain,
can fly directly to this part of Spain,
to this ferocious, natural work of art,
wind sculpture rising from each roundabout,
an immense, site-specific, installation-piece
parque temático; in the Manrique place,
a maker's cave and an obsidian mine
carved from the airy bubbles underground,
his own drawings, Tàpies and Joan Miró,
together with local work, are on permanent show.
The 'house' itself, art or ingenious kitsch
like a caged pontiff or a runny watch?

White-fronted civilization has made a stand
with tiered holiday flats above the sand

and rowdy beach parties on summer nights;
but it's precarious, for just inland
we've basalt rocks, boulders like meteorites
and, under the volcanoes, active furnaces
to remind us of the origins of the arts.
Do we need disaster to bring out the best,
calamity as a necessary precondition?
On 1 September, 1730, the Yaiza parish priest,
like the young Pliny writing from Pompeii,
was startled by a violent detonation,
an avalanche of lava, ash, debris,
a heavy rain of boiling condensation,
red hill ranges emerging from the earth
and searing dust storms, the great cosmic breath.

Sun worship, water sports; but Lanzarote,
much more than just a paradise for the yachtie
and windsurfer, provides an opportunity
to see things as they were and might be like:
low-lying life tucked into the landscape,
not only 'heritage' but a source of hope,
a civilization built on igneous rock
still cruel to the eye, hot to the touch,
formed from the dark interior of the globe
where cork and honeysuckle start from scratch
at dewfall, in the absence of other noise,
watched over by Nuestra Señora de los Remedios.
Maybe this was the world when it began,
slowly evolving myrtle, laurel, vine,
your backstroke in the white track of the sun;
but it's the old we notice in October —
the retired codger, brown as an almond, studying
the financial pages of the *Herald Tribune*,
sunk in a deckchair in his private dune;
the centenarian slowly wheeled along
the promenade; unhurried couples, sober

and reminiscent, of advancing age,
testing the temperature at the water's edge.

  After the holliers, no place for the young.
What irks me now at this end of the season
is wind and limb, cholesterol and gout
de-rhapsodizing the sun-lanced horizon,
the slowdown, with old age starting for real;
a bad back. When we get back to Kinsale
I sit late listening to an autumn wind
shaking the window, blowing leaves about
these northern gardens with an angry sound,
imposing chaos where I try to wring
form from the debris choking up the mind.
The equinoctial gales are overdue,
wind-banging door and moaning chimney flue.
Best practice recommends we let it be,
don't force the issue of formality,
yield to the natural shape on its own ground,
the rock formation; but the ancient rage
for order, the old curse, is too ingrained.
'Everything can be remedied', thyme and sage
redeemed from fire, the most unpromising
material shaped into a living thing
outlasting winter to a temperate spring.

Monochrome

The coat an uncle bought you as a girl —
tweed by the look of it, in a fifties style,
your blonde hair unfinicky and natural
lying in short waves round the hidden ears.
You're prematurely wise for eighteen years:
that level gaze, and that reserved smile!

A young idealist, your head in the wind,
before travel, sophistication and party time,
you're still living at home in Portballintrae
with its long winter nights and an extreme
cold that can do strange things to the mind,
reading the Brontës and Daphne du Maurier.

Soon enough you'll be in another town
picking out poets from the library shelves,
speaking in tongues, sporting a black gown
and spending your leisure hours with privileged
young gentlemen far too fond of themselves
where I first met you in another age.

Gowned like Czarinas, twirling parasols, you
and Sibyl stood at a roadside in Boulogne
hitching a lift to Greece; later you shone
on your own local afternoon talk show.
Too long a time in London, then the last
years spent on an obscure Indian quest.

Adored as a student, you never quite got over
the shock and glamour of your first lover.
Enamoured of high style, wounded by each
new manifestation of commercial kitsch,
you boggled at the crude, the daft, the naff
promoted by the genius of modern life . . .

This isn't good enough. I should make a list
of what you fancied: islands, freesia, fresh
strawberries, *broderie anglaise*, Schubert, snow;
the people, Maurice and Sandra, you liked best
and favourite phrases, 'kiddiewinks', 'cut a dash',
'a bit of zing', 'knee-trembler', 'the goat's toe'.

The cloudy backdrop gives you a period air
and sure enough you loved the cloudy past
so hard to revisit: how they really were,
the things they valued, obstacles *we* faced.
I can only half imagine how it was
to be a girl like you in the early days.

Pillow talk covered most of that I know
but in this monochrome, with little art,
the photographer in his Coleraine studio
caught the young woman I would know and love:
no speech, no fondly interrupted narrative
but the true nature and the secret heart —

as if I knew it, though you were my wife.
I walked on air but was too often drunk
till shouting started and we came undone
in a foreshadowing of the present grief.
When the crab grabbed and spread within
the chance had long gone to make up and thank

you for your forbearance, your anarchic laugh
and the grey gaze there in the photograph,
grey-blue in real life as it opened up
to wit and gaiety, to undying hope.
Dear ghost, remember me without ill will
as I remember your lost mystery still.

But don't mind me, for the important fact
is this, that you were once uniquely here,
a brief exposure, an exceptional act
performed once only in our slower lives
with your blue gaze and your longer hair
now ash for ever in the long sea waves.

Here in Tenerife

Winds light and easterly, decks damp with dew!
Provisioning here in Tenerife, he knew
he was on course, already on his way
to the riches of Chipangu and Quinsay.
Out there his cloud-sailed heaven ships
would find warm anchorage — perhaps;
out there beyond the shining sea
there would be cinnamon, antimony
and nightingales like Córdoba in May.

What if he'd lingered here and found only
aloe, cactus, a black beach? What if
he'd got no farther than this smoky cliff?
Dark ranges soared in the distance.
Would women hold him fast as long before,
or a bad omen, or persistent mist,
so his discoveries weren't out but in —
not gold and spices as in travel lore
but a soul voyage to the interior . . . ?

Goodbye, Columbus. Dogs turn from the tide
uninterested in new worlds, unexcited by
the thought of continents beyond the sky,
and light fading from rock and wrack
gives rise to a dead reckoning.
Day closes quickly at this latitude
as I too return the way I came
and gas brackets like planets climb
a shadowy path back up to the coast road.

The One-Thirty

The present generation sees everything clearly.
            — Gogol, *Dead Souls*

The one-thirty p.m. from Petersburg to Moscow
flashes past meadow, Gazprom and dusky forest
lit only by a twilight candle glow
in the days of revolution and civil war —
a dim vigil for history going sour,
the haunting spectre of a future lost;

and a thicket of aerials up an antique lane.
The ghostly whipped spire of a basilica,
spun blue and white, points to an arctic sky
as in the wilder days of Dostoevsky.
A tiny red light flickers off and on
like somebody smoking at a window sill

or a plane circling to land at Domodedovo.
No leaves left on suburban maple trees.
At the terminal a chill November breeze,
north-easterly, disperses the first snow,
white flurries hesitating too above
the crimson historic plaza where Lenin lies.

What history? Not the driven ones who work
at the huge desks, not strategy, not the dark
intrigues of the *ne kulturny* oligarch
so much as the slow thought of unknown powers,
wind stirring the wheatfields and wildflowers,
and the recurrent music of exemplars —

old folksong, Glinka and his first tutor
fresh from the west, magician of the keyboard,
tone poet of ice tinkle and frozen rain,
his slight sounds deliberate as thaw water
dropping at night, mysterious Field who 'Dead
in Moscow' from a surfeit of champagne.

Daily frustration and vindictive hunger
only intensified the songbirds' fever,
'Aesopian' in its deeply mined obliquity.
Sun dimmed and garden dripped; funereal weather
waited and listened for their silvery cry.
What doesn't kill you makes you stronger.

Icons, tractors, and this devotional urge
lives on in the profitable post-modern era:
dead souls still glistening like caviare,
the unrealized lives of Black Sea sturgeon
issuing finally in a playground song,
miraculous faces of the post-Soviet young.

The last survivors of the difficult years
have faces worn by hardship and lined by tears.
It's thanks to these, the sombre ones who suffered,
that the bright students can sip designer coffee.
'Let's go to the movies!', Voznesensky says;
but films are boring and inane these days.

Shandon Bridge

[rap]

She raps but nobody lets her in.
The winter nights are black as sin
though it isn't New York it's only Cork
where they distil the Cork Dry Gin.
So many things she might have done
but she's out of pocket she's out of luck
and just been dumped by her latest bloke.
Shake her and wake her on Shandon Bridge
as she tries to doze and the wind blows
like the cold breath of an open fridge.
She sits here in the 'knowledge' age
with a dirty face, an icy nose
and train lines up to her grimy elbows.
It's a great city, techno, noise,
the bases covered from folk to jazz
at the Red Star, the Quad, Crane Lane,
but she won't be getting on any train.
She's going to sit here in the rain
where some things are still real again
in a post-real world that scares her stiff.
Her thermal image glows with life,
a faint red-blue you can hardly see
by the dark flow of the lovely Lee.
A beautiful girl but what a sight
with her old jeans and her grungy look,
she barely survives amid the puke
without a home to call her own.
So many great things to be done
like making a video of her plight
or reading her poetry, open mic,
above the pub on a Monday night;
but here she sits where rain spits
at the pale, reflected river lights
and the future life looks void and vague.
She won't be going back home to Prague,

she won't be going back home to Kiev.
No, she's going to sit out here
in the rain till she can find the nerve
to look at the future long and clear
in the bright prism of a water drop.
The only direction left is up.

Cork Simon Community

Dreams of a Summer Night

The girls are quiet now in the house upstairs.
Still bright at ten with no need of music
on local habitations, tile and brick,
as the moon rises like a magic lamp
hung in a thorn bush and the sun retires
beyond the Bandon River; but I put on
young Mozart's Oboe Concerto, K.314,
the opening bit, in search of a nice tune —
and find it straight away, quick and exact,
the broken silence of the creative act.
Strangely, after the gold rush and the slump,
what remains is a great sense of relief.
Can we relax now and get on with life?
Step out and take a deep breath of night air
in peace, not having always to defer
to market forces, to the great hegemony,
the global hurricane, the rule of money?
High over Innishannon a single star
on the woods of this unthickly wooded shore.
Can we turn now to the important things
like visible scents, how even silence sings?
How we grew frolicsome one sunny June
some sixty years ago at Cushendun
in our young lives of clover, clock and cloud,
the first awakenings under a northern sky
heartbreaking in its extremity? 'One day
the old grow young,' as the old rock star said.

The first movement — *aperto*, open, frank —
declares its candour with a lively run
of oboe riffs; *adagio*, and we think
of the proactive soul in wind and wood
before revisiting the original mood
though more maturely, having lived meanwhile.
It's far from what Said meant by late style
since it was written by a twenty-year-old;
but I'm late listening, taking it all in

like a dreamt 'gentle concord' in the world.
Drilling for oil and war we seldom register
the resilient silence strewn about our toes
and under our very noses: thyme and sage,
mushroom and violet, briony, briar rose
and other elfin species. Soppy, I sniff
inchoate presences in the dim, substantive
trance of a summer night, its peace and quiet,
remembering poetry is a *real* mirage
in an unreal world of cash and babble,
iPod and car alarm, and remains 'a point of
departure not from reality but to it' —
wherein lies one function of the poet,
to be instrumental in the soul's increase.
During the May rising they used to say
«*Prenez vos désirs pour la réalité;
l'imagination au pouvoir!*» These very reasonable
demands are even more urgent for us today
trying to save ourselves from corporate space,
from virtuality with its image crime,
and Mozart from the ubiquitous pop sound:
fiddle and flute, soft oboe and clarinet,
the next best thing to silence in the mind,
that scarce but still renewable resource.
The young produce the liveliest work of course
but soon enough it's *Wild Strawberries* time,
age and experience, the lost summer house,
girls on a jetty, 'the old sunlit face'.

   There was a week of dreams for some reason,
some Kafkaesque and some more seasonable:
a concrete labyrinth with no obvious exit,
a maze of corridors, little natural light,
gruff notices prohibiting this and that,
no eating, drinking, smoking, and don't laugh,
surly administrative and security staff.
Alarms went off at intervals. Doors were shut

and windows, where there were windows, unopenable;
from secret offices a mysterious mumble
qualifying the air-conditioned silence:
Genetics, Human Resources, Behavioural Sciences.
Someone had proved the soul doesn't exist
and wiped out any traces of the past;
all were in danger but it faded fast
at the last minute, only to be replaced
by animations, eyes in a twitchy forest,
oak limbs outgrabbing, knuckles whitening, rock
speaking, Rackham *púcas* at face and neck.
These vanished too; then an erotic bower
snowed in by a warm leaf-and-petal shower
around the long ears and the bristling back.
She lay there in soft focus, her bright eye
moist with provocation; but just as I . . .

So many quiet shores 'bleared, smeared with toil',
there's nowhere for a sticky duck to hide
from the unchecked invasion of crude oil
dumped on the sand by a once friendly tide;
and if they drill here what else do we gain
but a bonanza for an acquisitive crowd
of blow-hard types, determined, garish, loud?
Would we ever get our old lives back again?
Gossip is history, history is gossip —
the locals talking in a hardware shop
about Tom Barry, James II, Marlborough
or that torpedo from a German sub,
the opening wine bar and the closing pub,
the pharmaceutical giant at Dunderrow,
its ethics, working conditions and so on,
a proposal to dig the whole town up again
for fibre optics and more 'information'
now on the table at the Kinsale borough
council and more than likely to go through.
'All politics is local', right where you are.

Communities are the real vehicles of power
not merely its last points of application
or they should be, says Amit Chaudhuri;
water and gas have first consideration
as every pre-Socratic thinker knew.
You hear a different music of the spheres
depending where you sit in the concert space,
so this is the centre of the whole creation:
important or trivial, it all finishes here
on your own starlit doorstep. It could be worse.

    A boreal sun, white nights of Petersburg!
The never fading gleam of Tír na nÓg!
But you can have too much of shiny things.
The dark has its own wisdom, its own owl-wings,
for this is when the spirits come out to play
and the grim ghosts we daren't admit by day.
Nacht und Träume: geese dreaming of maize,
old Ziggi's youngest crying out for 'stwawbewwies',
the entrepreneur with his elaborate schemes,
love dreams, exam dreams and anxiety dreams
'over-interpreted as they need to be.
I had a patient once . . .' But even he
granted the mystery of autonomous art,
those strange impulses circuiting the brain,
the plays of Shakespeare, symphonies of Mozart.

    Eleven and still light. No more music now
except for night and silence round the place.
Gazing into the past I hear once more
fathers and uncles back from a won war
and see 'the ice-cream on the pier', the rain
and windy picnics laid out under the brow
of the Cave Hill, Belfast laid out below —
then jump-cut to the dreams, vivid but short,
scaring us as they did when we were ten:
child murder in *Macbeth*, wolves at the door,

the dizzying height and the obscure disgrace,
indictments for a guilt we seldom face.
Sometimes you're hauled before a midnight court,
women presiding, to face charges of
failure in generosity, patience, love
and finer feeling. Often the chief judge
condemns you roundly to a change of heart
and sends you down abruptly for an age
of solitary. Read me the riot act again
in the grave, measured tone you used to restrain
my frantic idiocies. The least *I* can do
is praise your qualities the one way I know
now that I mourn, as here, your grace and poise,
your pungent wit, the laughter in your eyes,
the buoyant upbeat, the interior light
and those odd melancholy moments when
your head would close down with fastidious pain
at a world too coarse and tragic to be borne.
Aspiring spirit, late in finding rest
and harmony, may you have peace at last.
Today in a freak of thought I wondered if
the conservation-of-energy law applies
to souls and promises us eternal life.
At times like this we let ourselves imagine
some substance in the old claim of religion
that we don't die, not really. Don't light residues
commingle with the other starry dead
when our cold ashes in the earth are laid
or scattered on the waves at Port na Spaniagh
and the mad particles begin to spin
like sand grains in the night? Our contribution:
a few good books and a few words of caution.
You the unborn, the bright ones who come later,
remember we too sparkled in the sun,
burst on the shingle, perished underwater,
revolved our secrets in the vast oceans
of time, and live on in our transmigrations.

And you, old friend, Brancusi's 'Sleeping Muse',
who saved me when I'd nothing left to lose,
I can still wish for what you wish for too:
'the amazing truth 'tis no witchcraft to see',
refreshed tradition, lateral thought, a new
world politics and a disabused serenity.
These summer mornings I get up at five,
biro in hand, surprised to be still alive,
grateful for all the clichés and beguiled
by the first birdsong, the first light, the wild
relationship of water and cloud kingdoms
shaping our wishes and our waking dreams.
It's late, so lights out even as a last glow
still lingers on the gardens, on roof and rock:
mid-June now and it's never completely dark
but vague, ambrosial, metamorphic, slow
as if some happy mischief is at work
in the mist-pearly undergrowth below,
transfiguring the earth from dusk to dawn.

The moon floats from a cloud and two dogs bark;
the anthropomorphic trees are trees again,
the human forms recover their wood-grain
and the prehensile skins of hand and groin
revert, the limbs to branches, hair to leaves
as they resume their old arboreal lives.
The girls are fast asleep in the rooms above.
Back here from dreamland with a dewy leaf
to keep me right and ward off disbelief,
I await the daylight we were born to love:
birds at a window, boats on a rising wave,
light dancing on dawn water, the lives we live.

Indices of titles and first lines include also (in italics) parts of poems and sequences, many of which have been published separately.

Index of Titles

Index of First Lines